STUDENT

VEGGIE GRUB

Alastair Williams

SUMMERSDALE

First published in 1996
Reprinted in 2001

Available from

Summersdale Publishers
46 West Street
Chichester
West Sussex
PO19 1RP
United Kingdom

www.summersdale.com

A CIP catalogue record for this book
is available from the British Library.

ISBN 1 84024 186 1

Printed and bound by Creative Print and Design, Wales.

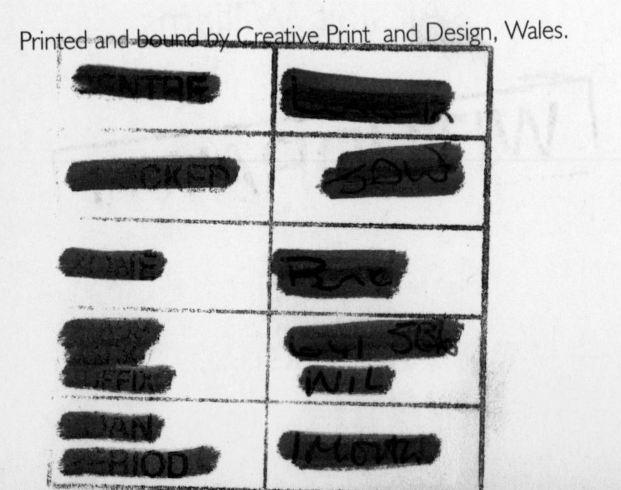

Contents

Introduction

Vegetarianism has a long pedigree. It was about forty million years ago that the first dinosaur decided to stop eating his friends and try eating his plants instead. Although this early attempt to spread the word failed, predictably, the cause of vegetarianism survived.

To be a vegetarian is no longer to be a pioneer. The range of recipes already in existence is so large that you can never grow tired of them. Vegetarian recipes exist for all types of dish: some try to emulate the original meat dishes on which they were based (such as Vegeburgers), others were invented as vegetarian dishes in the first place. The recipes in this book contain a balanced cross-section of the most popular recipes from each genre. All are designed to be easy and economical to cook, and therefore should be easily within the fiscal limitations of a student's income, within the technical limitations of a student's kitchen, and eventually within the recycling capacity of a student's lavatory.

If you've never cooked for yourself before, read the introductory sections of this book on the basics of cooking before you tackle any of the recipes (other than the sandwiches). Otherwise hire a chef for the next three years. Remember that university is not just about drinking and protesting at grant cuts. It is also about expanding your horizons, developing as a person, and learning to cope for yourself, which obviously involves cooking. Oh, and there's usually a bit of studying as well. This book won't help in your political protests or your studies, but if it goes some way towards giving you confidence in the kitchen, then it will have been worthwhile. If you also learn to cook great vegetarian food, then so much the better. But let's not run before we can walk.

The Rudiments

Being a good cook does not mean that you have to be able to create dazzling masterpieces every time you enter a kitchen. Even Van Gogh couldn't manage that. Learning how to cook is a gradual process that takes time and patience. The most experienced chefs still have occasional disasters . . . there was a great chef on the Titanic, for instance.

Remember that cooking is an art, not a science. You will find that even when you follow a recipe word for word it does not always turn out the way it should, there are many factors that affect the final result and you have to be aware of this. If you repeat a recipe several times over it is unlikely that it will ever taste or look exactly the same. With experience you will learn how to adapt recipes to your own tastes, skills and peculiarities.

One of the best ways of improving your cooking is to watch other cooks, preferably while they are cooking. This is where you pick up the little tricks and secrets that will enable you to increase your knowledge and skill. It is sensible to keep a small notebook so that you can jot down ideas and tips that you come across. Half the fun of cooking is in experimenting, using old skills and recipes and combining them with new ideas. The other half of the fun is washing up.

Kitchen Equipment

Any craftsman will have a set of tools that is essential to his trade. The same principle applies to the chef. There is a plethora of gadgets and gizmos on the market and it is very easy to believe that they are all essential; only when you see your cupboards bursting with juicers, sandwich-makers, blenders, steamers, yoghurt-makers, lager etc that you realise you have little room left for the food. Although some gadgets can aid the chef (speeding up laborious tasks such as chopping vegetables) others are dispensable and will soon find their way to the back of the cupboard after the novelty has worn off.

As a rule, it is far better to buy a few quality items than a number of inferior products. A frying pan that bends under the weight of a couple of eggs is going to be useless. Quality in cooking equipment often equates to weight, so a pan should have a thick bottom and a sturdy handle. However this does not mean that a saucepan so heavy that you need to start body-building before you can pick it up, is necessarily going to be the best.

Obviously the above rule will have to be broken if your budget won't extend to buying quality kitchen gear. The first alternative is to persuade someone to buy the stuff for you at Christmas. The other alternative is to get a cheap frying pan etc, and to make sure that when you toss, you do it gently. If the handle breaks, it could be messy.

Kitchen Knives

Investing in a quality set of knives is essential. Very few people have adequate kitchen knives, often relying on blunt flimsy instruments that are potentially dangerous. When choosing knives bear in mind for which job they are intended. It is sensible to have a selection of different sizes; it is not easy using a 10-inch blade for peeling fruit. I generally use just two sizes, a small cook's knife with a 3-inch blade, and a large 7-inch knife. It is also useful to have a serrated knife for cutting fruit. If you have the choice between buying a cheap set of knives or a couple of high quality knives, go for the latter.

The Freezer

The main advantage of having a freezer is that large quantities of food can be stored and used as and when required. If you arrive home late and are feeling too tired to cook then it is a joy to be able to go to the freezer and take out a ready-prepared meal. They can also save you time and money as food can be prepared and bought in bulk. When cooking a pasta sauce why not make double the amount, and freeze what is unused? A freezer is also useful for storing seasonal fruit and vegetables, so you can enjoy them any time of year. And don't forget plenty of soft scoop ice cream.

To aid fast freezing do not place large quantities of unfrozen food into the freezer at one go. This raises the temperature of the freezer and slows down the freezing process. Furthermore, food that has been cooked should be cold before being placed in the freezer.

If you are low on food or have an unexpected guest then don't panic; there should hopefully be something in the freezer that you can use. Or perhaps not. Do you actually know what is in your freezer and, perhaps more importantly, how long it has been there? It amazes me how many people's freezer contents lack any type of a labelling. It is often a case of lucky dip and then trying to guess by touch what has been so carefully wrapped up, which is no easy task when the items are frozen. I have heard these mystery items referred to as UFO's (unidentified frozen objects).

So it is essential that your freezer is organised: this will save you time and money.

It is a good idea to label and date all the items in your freezer. It is also handy to keep a separate list on the outside of the freezer door which you can update every time you add or remove something.

It is also worth remembering that freezers run more efficiently when they are full, so try to keep your freezer well stocked even if it is just half full of bread or your medic housemate's homework.

If you are going to make full use of your freezer then it is worth investing in a specific book that provides information on the different methods of preparing food for the freezer as well as telling you what can be frozen and for how long. Don't think that just because it is frozen you can necessarily retrieve a birthday cake that your mother made for you in 1985.

Sensibility

The recipes in this book are created with simplicity in mind, both in terms of implements and cooking skills required.Cooking can be a very sensual experience, with influences from both artistic and scientific domains. But don't forget that the element of common sense is most important of all (I don't want to be held responsible for a person who ends up in the hospital burns department for having misunderstood the instruction 'stand in boiling water for 20 minutes'!).

Another important point to remember is that all cooking times and temperatures are approximate. Not all ovens will take the same amount of time to cook a meal. If, for example, it is fan assisted you will have to allow for the extra efficiency. Cooking is ultimately intuitive and no amount of instructions can replace this. Before you try any recipe read through it first to make sure you have the ingredients and the time to prepare it.

The Kitchen

Just as a well-organised garage has a wide selection of high quality tools and adequate working space, the same applies to the kitchen. The purpose of a kitchen is to prepare food, therefore the element of hygiene must not be ignored. If you are a typical new student then it is perfectly understandable to want to show your independence by being as messy as possible but once you reach the stage where your overflowing bin touches the ceiling, however, make a note to sort it out before the end of term.

Although we usually have better things to do than worry about such trivialities as cleaning, I had better try to advocate virtuous behaviour, lest I become a target for irate flatmates. So, to keep everyone happy, good kitchen practice is to be recommended.

The three main areas are organisation, safety, and hygiene.

Organisation and Safety:

- Keep heavy items in the lower cupboards.
- Never use a stool to stand on whilst trying to reach an object. Even a chair can be unstable. So ideally you should have a small kitchen step ladder.
- The kitchen should be well ventilated so fumes and heat are removed quickly.
- There should be plenty of light, natural or artificial.
- A fire blanket and extinguisher should be kept handy.
- Keep cupboards tidy.
- Take care with the positioning of pans whilst cooking.
- Remember to keep the handles from protruding over the edge of the cooker.

- Make sure that handles on pots and pans are not loose.
- Keep an eye out for damaged flexes on electrical appliances such as toasters and kettles.
- Use caution when using electrical gadgets such as blenders and food processors.
- Keep matches and sharp knives out of reach from children.
- Knives should be kept sharp, as a blunt knife can slip when cutting and cause an accident.
- Kitchen knives should be kept in a knife block.Keeping them in a drawer not only causes the knives to lose their sharpness, it also makes it easier to cut oneself.
- Never learn to juggle using kitchen knives. Old socks filled with rice make a safer alternative. Any type of rice will do, except egg-fried rice.

Fat Fires:

- If you should experience a pan of oil igniting then remain calm and follow these rules.

- Never throw water on top of the oil as this will make it worse.

- Turn off the gas or electric hob if you can safely do so, otherwise wait until the fire has been extinguished.

- The most effective way to put out a oil fire is to get a dampened tea towel and place it over the top of the pan. Do not remove it for at least five minutes after the flames have subsided.

- If the fire is out of control, call the fire brigade and leave the house.

Hygiene

Not wishing to get into the gory details, being violently sick is usually a consequence of bad hygiene. Harmful bacteria can spread quickly in the right conditions, so here are a few guidelines.

- All surfaces such as worktops, floors and cookers should be cleaned regularly, and that doesn't mean just at the end of every term.

- Never let your kitchen surfaces get cluttered. Clean up as you go along. This makes food preparation easier as well as reducing the burden of washing-up at the end of the process. Let's face it no one likes this chore but it has to be done. I know the old excuse "I did the cooking, so someone else can do the washing up" is a good trick, but a good chef always clears up after himself as he goes along.

- Clean the door seals on fridges and freezers on a regular basis.

- Keep cooking utensils clean.

- Throw away food that is past its 'use by' date.

- Wash all fruit and vegetables.

You Want Me to do What?

Although some cooking terms might seem obvious there are probably many of you out there who will have trouble even finding the kitchen, let alone understanding recipe instructions!

Baste
To spoon fat or oil over food, in order to keep it moist.

Beat
This is the mixing of ingredients using a wooden spoon, a fork or a whisk.

Chop
To cut into small pieces.

Cream
To mix fat with a another ingredient such as sugar until it becomes creamy.

Dice
To cut into small cubes.

Grate
A grater can produce coarse or fine shavings of food, such as cheese or vegetables.

Knead
To use your knuckles to smooth dough out, the idea being to create a smooth texture.

Parboil

This is the partial boiling of something. The cooking will then normally be completed by another method. This applies, for example, to roast potatoes.

Peel

To the remove the skin or the outer layer of a vegetable or fruit.

Rub in

To rub flour and fat together between your fingertips until it resembles breadcrumbs.

Simmer

To cook just below boiling point, so that only an occasional bubble appears on the surface.

Order a Takeaway

To telephone for a pizza when your cooking goes disastrously wrong.

'roteins

'hese are referred to as the 'building blocks' of the body. Proteins re produced from a combination of amino acids and are found milk, cheese and eggs. Proteins are used to regenerate vital ormones such as insulin, adrenalin and thyroxin. A shortage of oteins results in poor growth or development of body cells.

itamins

is is one area where many people fail to supply their bodies rrectly. These are the most essential vitamins and their sources ong with some of the maladies that are incurred as a nsequence of the vitamin's absence.

amin A

amin A is present in dairy products such as cheese, butter d milk as well as in green vegetables. It is needed for growth, d resistance against disease.

amin B

min B is not one vitamin but a complex consisting of more n 16 different vitamins. They are to be found in whole grain eals and yeast.

min C

main source of the vitamin is citrus fruits (for example ons, oranges, and blackcurrants) and fresh vegetables. min C is needed for efficient functioning of the brain and ous system. It also increases our immune response to ctious diseases including the common cold.

min D

ficiency in vitamin D can lead to weak and brittle bones a lition known as rickets, which predominantly affects children.

Weights and Measures

There are certain things that indicate our age. Comments such as 'during the war' and 'I remember when this was all fields', are pointers as to our age. You might be asking 'what do fields and the war have to do with food?' Well not a lot, but somewhere in the mists of time the country went metric. Those imperial days are now long gone, but many people still prefer to think in imperial weights and measures, as I do myself. Hence the need to be able to convert metric to imperial and vice versa. Other amounts are referred to in spoons or cups which are self-explanatory.

The following abbreviations are used:

tbs = tablespoon tsp = teaspoon

If you don't possess a set of kitchen weighing scales then it is possible to convert certain ingredients into spoon measures. Obviously the weights of all ingredients will vary, but here are some rough measures . . .

1 tbs = 1 oz (25g) of . . . syrup, jam, honey etc
2 tbs = 1 oz (25g) of . . . butter, margarine, sugar
3 tbs = 1 oz (25g) of . . . cornflour, cocoa, flour
4 tbs = 1 oz (25g) of . . . grated cheese, porridge oats

All spoon measures refer to level spoons, not heaped.

1 tsp = 5ml
1 tbs = 15 ml

The approximations used for conversion between metric and imperial in this book are as follows . . .

1 oz	= 25g
2 oz	= 50g
3 oz	= 75g
4 oz	= 100g
6 oz	= 150g
8 oz	= 225g
1 lb	= 500g

¼ pint	= 150ml
½ pint	= 300ml
1 pint	= 600ml
2 pints	= 1 litre

Gas Mark	°C	°F
1	140	275
2	150	300
3	170	325
4	180	350
5	200	400
6	225	425
7	230	450
8	240	475
9	250	500

Healthy Eating

Healthy eating is the bugbear of the late twentieth and first centuries. Food gurus abound and every one of th different theory on what constitutes a 'healthy lifesty only water; eat only cabbage; hi-fibre; low-cholesterc

However the simple ket to achieving this heavenl dietry happiness is to adopt a *balanced* approach. O require certain elements (even fats) to achieve this:

Carbohydrates

These are the providers of energy and can predominantly in fruits, vegetables and grains.

Fats

If you are confused by all the talk about different types enlighten you. There are two basic types; satu unsaturated. The saturated fats are divided into poly and monounsaturated. It is these saturated fats that are to our health. Too much saturated fat can increase t of heart disease as the arteries become clogged, th the blood supply.

Although we should not overdo fat intake w without it. Fat is an important source of energy for fats take longer to digest than carbohydrates. This useful for storing energy. It is present in a variety of as butter, margarine, milk and cheese.

By looking at the fat content on packaging you much you are consuming. Low fat versions of man now available, although there is a tendency to reg inferior substitute to the 'real thing'.

In adults it can result in bow-legs. Thankfully this is a rarity now in this country. Vitamin D is found in milk, butter, and cheese.

Vitamin E

This is a vitamin that does not usually pose a deficiency problem in our society. It is found in milk, cheese, and butter. One of vitamin E's most important functions is that it helps to keep the blood from coagulating, thus preventing internal blood clots.

Vitamin K

This is found in green vegetables. It helps the blood clotting process, necessary for example after a break in one's skin.

Roughage

This is vital if you want to keep all your passages open, or if you are having trouble making substantial deposits. High fibre cereals provide a good source of roughage.

Water

It may seem obvious that the body requires a substantial amount of water in order to correctly function, but take this as a friendly reminder.

Minerals

There are three main minerals whose continued supply can all too easily be jeopardised: iron, calcium and iodine. Other minerals such as the phosphates, potassium, magnesium and sodium are generally in good supply.

Iron

This is vital for the formation of the red blood cells. If a person has a deficiency of iron it can lead to anaemia. This is a shortage of red blood cells. Women find they are more prone to this than men.

Calcium

This mineral is important for strong bones and teeth. It is found in dairy products.

Iodine

Iodine, although important, is not needed in the same quantities as calcium or iron.

Weights and Measures

There are certain things that indicate our age. Comments such as 'during the war' and 'I remember when this was all fields', are pointers as to our age. You might be asking 'what do fields and the war have to do with food?' Well not a lot, but somewhere in the mists of time the country went metric. Those imperial days are now long gone, but many people still prefer to think in imperial weights and measures, as I do myself. Hence the need to be able to convert metric to imperial and vice versa. Other amounts are referred to in spoons or cups which are self-explanatory.

The following abbreviations are used:

tbs = tablespoon tsp = teaspoon

If you don't possess a set of kitchen weighing scales then it is possible to convert certain ingredients into spoon measures. Obviously the weights of all ingredients will vary, but here are some rough measures . . .
1 tbs = 1 oz (25g) of . . . syrup, jam, honey etc
2 tbs = 1 oz (25g) of . . . butter, margarine, sugar
3 tbs = 1 oz (25g) of . . . cornflour, cocoa, flour
4 tbs = 1 oz (25g) of . . . grated cheese, porridge oats

All spoon measures refer to level spoons, not heaped.

1 tsp = 5ml
1 tbs = 15 ml

The approximations used for conversion between metric and imperial in this book are as follows . . .

1 oz	= 25g
2 oz	= 50g
3 oz	= 75g
4 oz	= 100g
6 oz	= 150g
8 oz	= 225g
1 lb	= 500g

¼ pint	= 150ml
½ pint	= 300ml
1 pint	= 600ml
2 pints	= 1 litre

Gas Mark	°C	°F
1	140	275
2	150	300
3	170	325
4	180	350
5	200	400
6	225	425
7	230	450
8	240	475
9	250	500

Healthy Eating

Healthy eating is the bugbear of the late twentieth and twenty-first centuries. Food gurus abound and every one of them has a different theory on what constitutes a 'healthy lifestyle': drink only water; eat only cabbage; hi-fibre; low-cholesterol . . .

However the simple ket to achieving this heavenly state of dietry happiness is to adopt a *balanced* approach. Our bodies require certain elements (even fats) to achieve this:

Carbohydrates

These are the providers of energy and can be found predominantly in fruits, vegetables and grains.

Fats

If you are confused by all the talk about different types of fats I will enlighten you. There are two basic types; saturated and unsaturated. The saturated fats are divided into polyunsaturated and monounsaturated. It is these saturated fats that are detrimental to our health. Too much saturated fat can increase the likelihood of heart disease as the arteries become clogged, thus impeding the blood supply.

Although we should not overdo fat intake we cannot do without it. Fat is an important source of energy for the body, but fats take longer to digest than carbohydrates. This means fat is useful for storing energy. It is present in a variety of products such as butter, margarine, milk and cheese.

By looking at the fat content on packaging you can see how much you are consuming. Low fat versions of many products are now available, although there is a tendency to regard them as an inferior substitute to the 'real thing'.

Proteins

These are referred to as the 'building blocks' of the body. Proteins are produced from a combination of amino acids and are found in milk, cheese and eggs. Proteins are used to regenerate vital hormones such as insulin, adrenalin and thyroxin. A shortage of proteins results in poor growth or development of body cells.

Vitamins

This is one area where many people fail to supply their bodies correctly. These are the most essential vitamins and their sources along with some of the maladies that are incurred as a consequence of the vitamin's absence.

Vitamin A

Vitamin A is present in dairy products such as cheese, butter and milk as well as in green vegetables. It is needed for growth, and resistance against disease.

Vitamin B

Vitamin B is not one vitamin but a complex consisting of more than 16 different vitamins. They are to be found in whole grain cereals and yeast.

Vitamin C

The main source of the vitamin is citrus fruits (for example lemons, oranges, and blackcurrants) and fresh vegetables. Vitamin C is needed for efficient functioning of the brain and nervous system. It also increases our immune response to infectious diseases including the common cold.

Vitamin D

A deficiency in vitamin D can lead to weak and brittle bones a condition known as rickets, which predominantly affects children.

In adults it can result in bow-legs. Thankfully this is a rarity now in this country. Vitamin D is found in milk, butter, and cheese.

Vitamin E

This is a vitamin that does not usually pose a deficiency problem in our society. It is found in milk, cheese, and butter. One of vitamin E's most important functions is that it helps to keep the blood from coagulating, thus preventing internal blood clots.

Vitamin K

This is found in green vegetables. It helps the blood clotting process, necessary for example after a break in one's skin.

Roughage

This is vital if you want to keep all your passages open, or if you are having trouble making substantial deposits. High fibre cereals provide a good source of roughage.

Water

It may seem obvious that the body requires a substantial amount of water in order to correctly function, but take this as a friendly reminder.

Minerals

There are three main minerals whose continued supply can all too easily be jeopardised: iron, calcium and iodine. Other minerals such as the phosphates, potassium, magnesium and sodium are generally in good supply.

Iron

This is vital for the formation of the red blood cells. If a person has a deficiency of iron it can lead to anaemia. This is a shortage of red blood cells. Women find they are more prone to this than men.

Calcium

This mineral is important for strong bones and teeth. It is found in dairy products.

Iodine

Iodine, although important, is not needed in the same quantities as calcium or iron.

The store cupboard

A well-stocked store cupboard is essential for any cook. Although a certain degree of improvisation is possible there are a number of basic ingredients that should always be kept in stock. It is a common problem when cooking that whatever ingredients you have in your cupboard will always be the things you don't need, while whatever you do need will be conspicuous by its absence. Here is a suggested list of useful things to have in your cupboard:

Tinned:

- Tomatoes *(used constantly throughout this book)*
- Sweetcorn
- Spaghetti
- Baked beans
- Chick peas
- Kidney beans
- Raspberries
- Peaches
- Pineapple pieces/rings
- Lager

Dry Goods

Cereals:
- Porridge oats

Flour:
- Self-raising
- Plain
- Cornflour

Custard Powder
Baking Powder
Biscuits

Pasta:
- Spaghetti
- Shells
- Lasagne
- Tagliatelli

Dried Fruits:
- Sultanas
- Currants
- Raisins
- Glace cherries

Nuts:
- Almonds
- Peanuts
- Walnuts

Rice:
- Long grain
- Basmati

Sugars:
- Castor
- Granulated or golden granulated
- Brown
- Icing

Coconut:
- Desiccated
- Soluble

Sauces:
- Tomato
- Worcester
- Tabasco
- Soy

Plain Chocolate

Oils and Vinegars

Buying habits have become much more exotic and sophisticated over the last decades. Foreign travel has meant that people are more likely to experience food from different countries and cultures. People also appear to have become more adventurous with what they eat. Where it would have once been impossible to find exotic foreign ingredients, such as baby sweetcorn or mangetout, they are now regarded as everyday products and are found in most supermarkets. The increased prevalence of such variety has meant that it is relatively easy to create authentic foreign cuisine.

In cooking there are a variety of oils that can be used. The most frequently used are blended vegetable oil, sunflower oil, corn oil and olive oil. Each of the oils is very different in flavour so experiment with each type to see which flavour you prefer. There is no doubt that the most highly prized of those oils is olive oil. Olive oil experts are a little like wine experts: they can tell by taste the origin of a particular oil, be it *Shell*, *Castrol* or plain *3-in-1*.

The majority of olive oil we use comes from France, Italy, Spain or Greece. The oil is produced by the pressing of the olives. The first cold pressing produces the best quality oil which is called Extra Virgin Olive Oil. The olives are then pressed again to produce a lower quality oil and a corresponding price. Olive oil is not the sort of oil in which you would fry chips, it is expensive and inappropriately flavoured. However olive oil can't be beaten for French dressings, or mayonnaise. Other more unusual oils include walnut oil which can be used in salads to add a nutty flavour, or Sesame seed oil which is used in Chinese cuisine.

Vegetables

Below is a list of some of the common and not-so-common vegetables currently available, explaining how they should be prepared and various methods of cooking.

Artichokes (Globe)

These are interesting vegetables in terms of shape and texture. If you are buying artichokes make sure they look fresh with no brown tinges to the leaves, if the leaves are drying out leave them.

Before cooking remove a few of the tough outer leaves, cut off the stalks, and then wash. Place in a pan of salted boiling water, reduce the heat to a simmer and continue to simmer until an outside leaf can be removed with ease. This should take about 30 minutes, depending on the size and age of the artichoke.

Drain well and serve. To eat an artichoke it is advisable to use one's fingers. Remove any remaining leaves to expose the tender ones. Dip in melted butter, then eat the fleshy part of the leaf, discarding the rest. The treasured piece of the artichoke is the heart which is found at the bottom of the leaves. Don't eat the fluffy centre which tastes like a carpet.

As an alternative serve them cold with a Vinaigrette dressing.

Asparagus

This is not your everyday vegetable, but it is well worth splashing out on once in a while. Use asparagus as soon it is bought, or as soon as you get home if you're not allowed to cook in the supermarket car park. When buying asparagus pick bundles that contain heads of the same size.

To prepare, untie the bundles. Remove 1 or 2 inches off the stalk. Using a small knife scrape downwards to remove the outer layer. Wash and tie back into bundles. Place the asparagus in a deep pan and simmer for about 10 minutes or until tender. Serve straight away with either butter, mayonnaise or hollandaise sauce.

Aubergine/Eggplant

There are a number of varieties, but the most common are purple in colour. When buying aubergines choose those with a firm skin. Cut the top and bottom off and then slice thinly. Before cooking it is normal to extract the bitter juice that is present. Sprinkle lightly with salt and leave for 20 minutes. Before cooking, rinse the slices in water, then pat dry with a paper towel. The usual method for cooking aubergines is to fry them either in oil or butter until they soften.

Baby Sweetcorn

This expensive import from the Orient is worth the price. The only preparation needed is washing, following which they can be gently boiled or fried. To benefit from their full flavour they need to retain their crispness, so don't over-cook.

Beans (French)

Wash them and top and tail. Cut into 1-inch lengths, or leave whole. To cook, place in boiling salted water and cook for 10 to 15 minutes. After cooking they can be tossed in butter.

Broccoli

Wash in cold water. Cut off the stalks then divide into flowerets, ie. into clumps. Place in boiling water for about 10 minutes. Don't over-cook as it will cause the broccoli to become mushy losing most of its flavour and colour.

Brussels Sprouts

Remove the outer leaves and cut off the stalk. It should not be removed entirely, otherwise all the leaves will fall off. Cut a cross into the base and then wash in cold water. Boil in water with a pinch of salt for 10 minutes.

Cabbage

Remove the rough outer leaves and the centre stalk. You can either shred or quarter the leaves. To cook the shredded cabbage place in boiling water for about 5 minutes. If the leaves are bigger they will need about 10 minutes.

Carrots

Top and tail the carrots and then either using a scraper or a knife remove the outer surface. Before cooking they can be quartered or sliced. Baby carrots can be cooked whole. Boil in salted water for 15 to 20 minutes. Carrots can be eaten raw in salads etc. They can also be roasted in oil when cooking a roast dinner.

Cauliflower

Wash in cold water and then divide into flowerets. Boil in salted water until tender — this should take about 10 minutes depending on the size of the flowerets. Cauliflower can also be eaten raw and used as a crudité.

Courgettes

Having been force-fed these for years I have almost come to like them. First of all give them a wash, then top and tail them. Slice thinly and fry in butter or oil for about 5 minutes. Alternatively boil for approximately 5 minutes.

Leeks

Remove the dark green section of the stalk and the roots and wash. They can either be sliced into rings, quartered or even left whole. To cook either boil for 10 to 15 minutes or fry in oil or butter for about 10 minutes.

Mangetout

If you haven't seen these before, they look like pea pods that have been squashed by a lorry. But they taste delicious and are arguably worth the extortionate amount you will be charged for them.

To prepare your mangetout, wash them, then top and tail. If boiling, they need only 3 or 4 minutes because they maintain their flavour better when still crisp. They can also be fried gently in butter for a few minutes until they soften slightly. They make a colourful addition to stir fries.

Mushrooms

The many types of mushroom available, range from the standard button variety to the more exotic oyster or shittaki. Some mushrooms can be eaten raw but always wash them first by wiping with a damp cloth. Either remove or trim the stalk and then slice or leave whole. The mushrooms can be fried or grilled. To fry, melt a little oil or butter in a frying pan and cook for about 3 to 4 minutes, depending on size. To grill, put under a hot grill with a light covering of butter. Mushrooms can be a great addition to many sauces.

Onions

The best way to stop your eyes watering when chopping onions is to get someone else to do it. Top and tail the onion first and peel off the outer layer. It can then be chopped vertically or sliced into rings. Onions are normally fried in oil for about 5 minutes. They can be boiled in salted water for about 10 minutes. When frying onions take care that you don't burn them as this can taint a whole meal even if only a few of the onions are burnt.

Parsnips

Top and tail, then peel and chop into largish pieces or thick slices. They can be boiled, fried or roasted.

Place in boiling water with a pinch of salt for about 20 minutes or until they are tender.

If they are to be fried they need to be cut into thin slices or chips, otherwise they will not cook all the way through.

Perhaps the nicest way of cooking parsnips is to bake them. Place the parsnips in an ovenproof dish with a couple of tablespoons of oil, and bake in a hot oven for about 40 minutes. They can be basted as if they were roast potatoes.

Peas

If you have fresh peas, ie. still in the pod, shell them and wash in cold water. To cook the peas, place them in boiling water for about 10 minutes.

Peppers

Available in red, green, yellow and orange. They all have different flavours – the lighter in colour, they are the sweeter they are; so the yellow ones are the sweetest and the green ones the most bitter. Top and tail, then remove all the core and seeds. Slice into rings then halve and fry in a little oil for 5 minutes or so.

Potatoes

Just as the Italians have their pasta, we seem to be mad about potatoes. We serve them in various guises, be it chips, crisps, roasted, boiled or mashed.

There are two basic types of potato: 'new' and 'old'. Both are available all year round, although new potatoes are cheaper in the summer. Allow 1 or 2 potatoes per person, depending on your appetite, the size of the potato, and the size of the person.

All potatoes need to be peeled or scrubbed before cooking, unless you are preparing jacket potatoes.

Boiled Potatoes

After peeling or scrubbing the potato, cut into halves or quarters, depending on its size, then place in salted boiling water for 15 to 20 minutes or until they are tender all the way through.

Mashed Potatoes

If you want mashed potato make sure they are well cooked, you should be able to pass a knife through them easily. If they are not well cooked you find that the mashed potatoes have lumps in, however hard you try to remove them. Drain the potatoes, add a nob of butter and a drop of milk, then using a potato masher squash until they are nice and creamy, adding more milk and black pepper if required.

Roast Potatoes

There are a number of ways to produce roast potatoes. Obviously having a potato and an oven is a good starting point. As with most recipes personal preference tends to dictate what method is used. I prefer small crisp potatoes and will settle for nothing less. Peel the potatoes, then halve or quarter them depending on their size. Parboil for 5 minutes in salted boiling water, then drain. Drain the potatoes in a colander and shake so that the surfaces of the potatoes are slightly flaky (this produces crisp edges). Place the semi-cooked potatoes in a baking tray with some oil and place in the oven on Gas Mark 6 (425 °F, 220 °C) near the top of the oven if possible. Baste the potatoes with the oil a couple times while they are cooking. Roast the potatoes until they are golden and verging on crispiness, this should take between 60 and 90 minutes.

Chips

Peel some old potatoes and cut into chip shapes. If you are feeling sophisticated slice them thinner into French fries. The next stage is potentially dangerous so take care. The chips need to be covered or at least partially covered in oil to cook, so a large amount of oil is needed.

Heat the oil in a large frying pan. To test if the oil is hot enough drop one chip in — if the oil bubbles loudly all around the chip it is up to temperature. Carefully add the chips, taking care not to throw them in the pan, otherwise hot oil will be splashed.

Fry the chips until they are crisp, making sure that the oil does not get too hot.

Remember to turn the heat off as soon as you have finished frying.

Pumpkin

If you have a whole pumpkin, cut it into 4 pieces then remove all the seeds and pulp from the inside. Remove the skin and cut into chunks. To boil, place in salted boiling water for about 30 minutes.

After the pumpkin has been boiled it can be fried in butter for 5 minutes.

Spinach

When buying spinach, buy more than you think you need as spinach will shrink considerably during cooking. Discard any yellowed leaves, then place in a small amount of boiling water for about 10 minutes. Grated nutmeg and spinach taste good together.

Swede

Peel and chop into chunks, then wash in cold water. Cook in salted boiling water for 20 to 25 minutes or until tender. Can be mashed with a nob of butter and black pepper.

Sweetcorn

Remove the husks and the ends, then place in boiling water for 10 minutes. Drain, then serve with butter and fresh black pepper.

Tomato

Fresh tomatoes can be fried in butter, grilled or baked. To remove the skin of a tomato, which should be done when making sauces, place in boiling water for about a minute. Remove from the hot water and cool them in cold water. The skins should now come away with ease.

Turnip

Peel and cut into chunks, then place in boiling water for 20 to 25 minutes or until tender.

Spices, Herbs, Seasonings and Flavourings

Cooking without herbs and spices is like looking at the world in black and white, having a bath without any water, or going out without a hat. Given moderate use, spices, herbs and seasonings can transform a plain tasting meal into something special. Spices from around the world are available in most supermarkets, so it is possible to recreate authentic cuisine from as far afield as Thailand to Torquay. Just remember the amounts used have to be carefully controlled, the idea being to enhance the flavour of the food, not to annihilate your taste buds. Many spices are available in different strengths such as chilli and curry powder, and there is sometimes a difference between brands, so go on the side of caution.

When the recipes say salt and pepper it generally means a pinch of each, but it is up to the individual to season according to taste. One of the most essential items in a kitchen is a pepper mill. Freshly ground pepper tastes so much better than the pre-ground stuff. If you wish to cut down on your salt intake use a salt substitute, there are several on the market.

If you have a garden why not grow your own herbs? Mint, rosemary, sage, thyme and sorrel all flourish in our climate. Basil does not fair so well lacking the intense flavour that is found from the imported product.

Garlic

Whenever the word garlic is mentioned it provokes the same old comments about smelly breath and how useful it is for keeping vampires away. What they should be talking about is how it is one of the most vital ingredients in cooking. Garlic is related to the onion. Although normally associated with France it is believed that it originated in Asia, where it is still used in abundance. As well as the white skinned garlic it can also be found with a pink or even light purple covering. The only difference is that they seem to taste a little milder than the white.

When choosing garlic look for firm undamaged bulbs. Should you see any sign of green shoots appearing from the top of the bulb, don't buy it. Garlic should be stored in a dry place, and although hanging it in the kitchen may provide the kitchen with bit of rustic charm it is not the ideal place, as the temperature fluctuates, and there is a high degree of moisture. Special terracotta garlic pots are good if you are only keeping small quantities.

When using garlic it is a matter of preference as to how much is used, depending on the required flavour of the dish. It is not only the amount of garlic that is used that will affect how strong the taste of garlic will be, the method of preparation and cooking of the garlic will also contribute.

A subtle addition can be made to a salad by rubbing the inside of a salad bowl with a clove of garlic. When garlic is uncooked and used raw it is in its most powerful state; cooking garlic reduces its potency. Garlic can be sliced, chopped, or crushed according to the flavour required. Slicing gives the most mild effect, then chopping and finally crushing. Devices such as garlic presses are useful but I find that they are a bind to clean thoroughly.

Stocks

Although it is easy to be tempted into using a stock cube, you'd be surprised at the improvement in a recipe that uses fresh stock, especially in soups and casseroles. They can also be frozen in ice cube trays, so that the amount used can be carefully controlled and used as and when required.

Savoury Sauces

There is the potential for an almost unlimited number of sauces, and they can be used to brighten up a plain tasting dish or act as a harmonious accompaniment. The many sauces are based on a small number of elementary ingredients and once the fundamentals are mastered the possibilities are infinite. Not all sauces are simple, in fact some are downright difficult, so patience is imperative and a little confidence is helpful. The secret to a successful sauce is not to rush it, avoid short cuts, and don't jump the lights.

Cheese Sauce

This sauce is used in many of the recipes in this book, such as lasagne or cauliflower cheese.

Ingredients

½ pint (300ml) of milk
2 oz (50g) of grated cheese
¾ oz (20g) of butter
¾ oz (20g) of plain flour
Salt
Pepper

Repeat the method as for the white sauce, except after the sauce has been brought to the boil add the cheese. Stir in the cheese, then simmer until it has completely melted.

White Sauce

Ingredients

¾ oz (20g) flour
½ pint (300ml) milk
1 oz (25g) butter
Salt
Pepper

Melt the butter in a small saucepan, but don't let it brown. Then stir in the flour and cook gently for a couple of minutes. The combination of butter and flour is called a roux, and it is also the name of the method of preparation.

Remove the roux from the heat and add a little of the milk. It has to be added gradually otherwise it will end up being lumpy. Stir the milk in until a smooth consistency is achieved, then progressively add the rest of the milk. When all the milk has been added return the pan to the heat and bring to the boil. Simmer for 3 to 5 minutes or until the sauce has thickened, stirring the sauce as it cooks. Season as required.

Mayonnaise

Once you have made your own mayonnaise you will be loathe to return to the prefabricated variety: there is no comparison. An added bonus is that once you have mastered making mayonnaise you can go on to make aioli. This Provençal speciality is totally moreish, the only dilemma is that its main flavouring is garlic!

Ingredients

2 egg yolks
2 tsp of white wine vinegar
½ pint (300ml) of olive oil
Squirt of lemon juice
1 tsp of smooth French mustard
Salt
Pepper

Put the egg yolks into a mixing bowl with the mustard and mix together. Then slowly begin to add the olive oil. The main problem with making mayonnaise is that it can curdle if the oil is added too quickly. Mayonnaise is time consuming to make and it is essential to take care. A fine drizzle of oil is needed and has to be controlled with total precision; hold the bottle of oil at the bottom in the palm of your hand, this gives more control. Using a balloon whisk, beat the yolks and the oil together. You will notice that the colour is quite yellow in comparison to the bought variety, but this is the way it should be. Keep whisking the mayonnaise until all the oil is added, then add the vinegar, lemon juice, salt, pepper and mix. Taste and adjust the flavourings to suit.

This is making mayonnaise the hard way, and if you are making larger quantities you will be quite exhausted by the time you have finished. There is an alternative. Mayonnaise can be produced in a food processor, but again fine control is required and the result is not as good. Put all the ingredients, bar the oil, in the processor and switch on, then add the oil slowly.

Pesto

This recipe uses insane quantities of fresh basil, but the aroma is intoxicating. Pesto is traditionally served with pasta, but it can be spread on toast.

Serves 4

Ingredients

2 cloves of garlic, peeled and crushed
2 oz (50g) of pine nuts
2 cups of fresh basil leaves
3 tbs of finely grated fresh parmesan
¼ pint (150ml) olive oil
Salt

Put the basil leaves, pine nuts and the garlic in a blender and grind for a few seconds. Then add the cheese, oil and salt and mix well. If you are a stickler for authenticity, then you should prepare the pesto in a mortar, but a blender is far quicker.

Parsley Sauce

Ingredients

½ pint (300ml) milk
¾ oz (20g) of plain flour
¾ oz (20g) of butter
4 tbs of chopped fresh parsley
Salt
Pepper

As White Sauce. The parsley is added just before serving.

Bread Sauce

One of the top sauces, up there with cranberry sauce and similar in many respects, except that it hasn't got any cranberries in it.

Ingredients

4 oz (100g) fresh white breadcrumbs
1 oz (25g) butter
¾ pint (400ml) milk
1 onion, peeled
4 cloves
4 peppercorns
Pinch of nutmeg
1 bay leaf
Salt
Pepper

Cut the onion in two and press the cloves into the onion. Place the onion in a saucepan with the milk, bay leaf, nutmeg and peppercorns.

Bring to the boil then remove from the heat and leave to infuse for 15 minutes. Strain into a bowl then pour over the breadcrumbs. Mix in the butter then return to the pan and heat until the sauce thickens.

Aioli

This is one Provençal recipe that lacks the characteristic vibrant colours normally associated with its cuisine. What it might lack in colour, however, it makes up for in flavour. This recipe packs more of a punch than Mike Tyson. It is rarely served in this country, possibly as a result of its high garlic content. You are missing out if you don't try this favourite of our Gaelic chums. Aioli should ideally be served with freshly cooked vegetables such as courgettes or French beans and also tastes great with hard-boiled eggs and raw tomatoes. Serve on a large platter dish.

Ingredients

6 cloves of garlic
2 egg yolks
Juice of 1 lemon
½ pint (300ml) of olive oil
Salt
Pepper

Using a pestle and mortar crush the garlic with pinch of salt into a fine paste. If you don't have a pestle and mortar improvise using a small bowl and the back of a spoon.

Transfer the garlic into a mixing bowl then add the egg yolks. The next stage is the same as when making mayonnaise; the oil must be added very slowly and be stirred constantly. When all the oil is added, season and add the lemon juice.

Barbecue Sauce

I tend to make barbecue sauces out of whatever is to hand. A little of this and that can provide some interesting results. Remember to taste the sauce before you cover your food with it, just to be safe.

Ingredients

4 tbs olive oil
1 tbs honey
2 tbs tomato purée
1 garlic clove, peeled and crushed
1 tsp tabasco
1 tsp Worcester sauce
2 tbs wine vinegar
2 tsp corn flour

Heat the oil in a small saucepan, then add the other ingredients stirring constantly. Make sure that all the ingredients are thoroughly mixed. Remove from the heat and cool. If you want to be a little more adventurous try adding other ingredients such as chutney, mustard, herbs or soy sauce.

Cranberry Sauce

Christmas. Humbug! I must confess to not being the biggest fan of Christmas. Too many relatives, silly paper hats, noise and commotion, then there's the shopping. There are, I suppose, a few minor compensations: the inevitable repeats of Star Wars and Chitty Chitty Bang Bang to keep us amused, and an excuse to eat copious amounts of food, accompanied by attempts to drink the country dry. At the end of the festivities you are normally left fat, broke and with a hangover that will probably stay until the Christmas carols start playing in the shops reminding us that there are only 200 shopping days until next Yuletide.

Ingredients

8 oz (225g) fresh cranberries
½ pint (300ml) water
4 oz (100g) sugar

Boil the water in a large saucepan then add the cranberries. Cook for about 15 minutes or until they are tender. Stir in the sugar and heat through until the sugar has dissolved. If a thinner sauce is required add a little more water.

Mint Sauce

Ingredients

Cup of fresh mint
2 tbs vinegar
2 tbs castor sugar
2 tbs hot water

Wash the mint then remove the leaves. Finely chop the leaves and place in a bowl with the sugar. Pour on the hot water and stir. Leave for 5 minutes or until the sugar has dissolved. Add the vinegar and leave to infuse for at least 2 hours.

Apple Sauce

Ingredients

1 lb (500g) cooking apples, peeled, cored, sliced
3 tbs of water
Juice of half a lemon
½ oz (15g) butter
2 tsp of sugar

Put the apples in a saucepan with the lemon juice, water, sugar and butter and simmer gently until the apples are soft. Take care not to burn the apples. If you want a smooth sauce put the mixture in a blender for a minute. If the sauce is too bitter add a little more sugar. To make the sauce a little special add a tablespoon of calvados.

Dressings

The use of dressings can add life to even the most miserable salad. Even fresh peppers dunked in a little olive oil would constitute a dressing. By making your own dressings you can fine-tune them according to your own personal tastes. It should be remembered that a dressing should not swamp a salad. The salad should be coated not bathed. It is possible to buy ready prepared dressings but they rarely match those that are homemade.

French Dressing

There are many variations of French dressing, and most people have there own favourite combinations. Oil and vinegar are the primary ingredients to which herbs or flavourings can be added.

As with most recipes, even ones that only contain two ingredients, there are disagreements as to the correct proportions of oil and vinegar. This is yet another one of those daft arguments: the proportions should simply be based upon personal preference. In theory the average is 4 parts oil to 1 part vinegar, but I'm not advocating this as a fixed rule. You might prefer a less acidic flavour and use 6 parts oil, and so on.

Ingredients

4 tbs olive oil
1 tbs white wine vinegar
Salt
Pepper

What could be easier? Put the oil, vinegar, salt and pepper in a small screw top jar and shake until the two liquids have combined. After a while the oil and vinegar will separate again.

If you want a dressing out of the ordinary try adding a little mustard or fresh herbs such as basil, mint, parsley or chives. An alternative to using vinegar is to use lemon juice.

Garlic Dressing

Make as above, but add half a finely crushed clove of garlic.

Yoghurt Dressing

Yoghurts are renowned for their lack of inhibition, so no need to look away.

Ingredients

¼ pint (150ml) of plain yoghurt
1 tbs of lemon juice
Salt
Pepper

Mix the yoghurt and lemon juice together, season according to taste.

Dips and savoury butters

Humous

This is a dip of Middle Eastern origin and is easy to make. Although humous is available ready-made, it is cheaper to make your own. Having said that, I find it easier to use canned chick peas instead of soaking dried ones for hours. Serve with pitta bread.

Note that a blender is needed for this recipe.

Ingredients

1 can of chick peas
2 cloves of garlic, peeled and finely chopped
1 tbs of tahini
Juice of one lemon
2 tbs of olive oil
½ tsp of ground cumin
Paprika

Put all the ingredients in a blender and let them have it! Switch off when a smooth consistency has been achieved. Then put in a dish and chill for an hour or two. Before serving dust with paprika.

Cucumber Raita

Serves 2 to 4

Ingredients

½ cucumber, peeled and chopped into pieces
1 small pot of natural yoghurt
1 tbs of olive oil
1 tbs of freshly chopped mint
Pepper
Salt

Mix the cucumber, yoghurt and mint together in a bowl, pour the oil on top, and season.

Garlic Butter

Not only is this the crucial ingredient for 'garlic bread', it can also be used with vegetables.

Ingredients

4 oz (100g) butter
2 cloves of garlic, peeled and crushed
Salt
Pepper

Beat the ingredients together.

Guacamole

Originally from Central America, this is a variety of mole that lives deep below ground, and is rarely responsible for the lumpy lawn damage so often attributed to them. They are remarkably short sighted, so pulling silly faces at them has no effect on their bubbly personas.

Ingredients

2 ripe avocados
3 tbs lemon juice
1 tbs olive oil
1 clove of garlic, peeled and crushed
Pinch of chilli powder
Salt
Pepper

Peel the avocados and remove the stones. Mash the flesh with a fork and add the other ingredients. Season to taste and serve with tortilla chips, raw vegetables or on toast.

Starters

Many of these recipes do not have to be served as a starter, the amounts can be increased so they can be served as a main meal.

Deep Fried Camembert

There is another recipe that involves baking a whole Camembert in the embers of a fire. See the chapter on barbecues.

Serves 2

Ingredients

Vegetable oil
1 camembert cheese
Dried white breadcrumbs
1 egg, beaten

Cut the camembert into four then dip in the egg, followed by a roll in the breadcrumbs, making sure they are evenly coated. Put on a plate and place in the fridge for 30 minutes.

Heat the oil in a deep fryer until it begins to smoke. Test the temperature by dropping a breadcrumb into the oil: it should sizzle as soon as it hits the surface. When the oil is at the correct temperature fry the camembert until golden. Drain and then serve with redcurrant sauce.

Cinnamon Toasted Grapefruit

This is a very quick and tasty way of serving grapefruit.

Serves 2

Ingredients

1 grapefruit
2 tsp of soft brown sugar
1 tsp of butter
½ tsp of cinnamon

Cut the grapefruit in half and remove the pips. Loosen the segments using a grapefruit knife. Put 1 tsp of brown sugar on each half with the butter and a light sprinkling of cinnamon. Place under a hot grill for 5 minutes.

Garlic Bread

Garlic bread is even more popular than the toilet at student parties, and is easier to clean up.

Ingredients

French stick
4 oz (100g) of butter
2 cloves of garlic
Tinfoil

Put the butter in a small mixing bowl. Finely chop the garlic and add to the butter, blending it in with a fork. Slice the French stick at 2-inch intervals, without actually severing it, and spread some of the butter on both sides of each slit. Then close up the gaps and wrap the loaf in foil. Place in the oven and cook for 15 to 20 minutes at Gas Mark 5 (400 °F, 200 °C).

Courgette Fritters

This is a well known and loved Italian dish that makes an excellent starter or snack. They should be eaten as quickly as possible after cooking: the last one to finish washes up.

Serves 4

Ingredients

1 lb (500g) courgettes
Vegetable oil
2 egg whites
Plain flour
Salt
Pepper

Cut the courgettes into matchsticks and sprinkle with salt. Leave for 30 minutes, then wash, drain and dry. Season the flour with the salt and pepper. Whisk the egg whites in a bowl until they go stiff. A mixer will make this job a lot easier than using a hand-whisk.

Heat the oil in a large frying pan until it begins to smoke. When the oil is up to temperature put the courgettes in a sieve and add the flour. When they are coated in the flour remove and dip in the egg white. Fry a few at a time until they are golden brown.

Mung Bean Paté

Mung beans are ideal for this recipe: jumping beans make a poor substitute because they get stuck in the paté.

Serves 4

Ingredients

4 tbs olive oil
8 oz (225g) mung beans
4 oz (100g) ricotta cheese
3 tbs chopped parsley
1 pint of water
2 onions, peeled and chopped
1 clove of garlic, peeled and finely chopped
Juice of one lemon

Before cooking the beans they need to be soaked overnight.

Having soaked the beans place in large saucepan with the water. Bring to the boil then simmer for 40 minutes. Whilst the beans are cooking, heat the oil in a large frying pan. Gently cook the onions and garlic for about 8 minutes. Be careful not to burn the onions as the paté will taste awful.

Transfer the beans and lemon juice into the frying pan and mix, cooking gently for a few minutes. Put the bean mixture into a blender and give it a whizz for a few seconds depending on how smooth you require your paté.

Stir in the ricotta and the parsley then place in a dish or mould. The paté needs to be refrigerated for at least 4 hours before serving.

Mushrooms with Garlic Butter

Mushrooms love to be covered with garlic butter — they feel naked without it. Only inferior quality mushrooms will accept margarine as a substitute.

Ingredients

4 oz (100g) of mushrooms
3 oz (100g) of butter
2 cloves of garlic, peeled and finely chopped

Remove the stalk of the mushrooms then wash. Mix the butter and the garlic together with a fork and then spread on top of the mushrooms. Bake in the oven for 15 minutes on Gas Mark 5 (400 °F, 200 °C).

Goat's Cheese Salad

If you are into strong cheese, then a ripe goat's cheese can bring tears to your eyes, if not to the goat's. There are many ways of serving goat's cheese, apart from the obvious bread accompaniment. It is sometimes served with fresh figs, or in a salad.

Serves 4

Ingredients

4 small goat's cheeses
Mixed salad
2 tps of olive oil
Salt
Pepper

Arrange the salad on four small plates. Heat the oil in a small frying pan and then add the cheese. Lightly fry the cheese until it gets close to melting. Use a pan slice to remove it from the heat and then place on top of the salad. Any oil that remains in the pan can be poured over the salad. Finally season.

Soups

The recipes for soup are legendary. There are thick, thin, clear, hot, cold and it is possible to produce soup from almost any natural ingredients. A blender is essential if you want a smooth soup. Soups are ideal for freezing so why not make double the quantity and freeze what you don't use?

Carrot and Ginger Soup

This is my favourite of all soups, the ginger gives it a delicious flavour that never fails to impress. Use fresh ginger, but remember to take it out before serving.

Serves 4

Ingredients

1 lb (500g) carrots, peeled and chopped
1 potato, peeled
1 piece of fresh root ginger, peeled and chopped
2 pints (1 litre) water
4 tbs single cream (optional)
Salt
Pepper

Place the carrots, potato and ginger in a pan and cover with the water. Bring to the boil and then simmer for 20 minutes. Remove from the heat and take out the ginger. Transfer the ingredients into a blender and blend until a smooth consistency is achieved. Season according to taste and stir in the cream if desired.

Potato and Leek Soup

The traditional method of preparing this dish is first to hollow out the potato with a small spoon, pour in about a potato-full of soup, then prick the potato skin with a fork. Finally, hold the potato up above your head and admire the leak.

Serves 4

Ingredients

I large leek
2 potatoes, peeled and chopped into quarters
I pint of vegetable stock
2 tbs cream
I oz (25g) butter
Salt
Pepper

Wash the leek thoroughly then top and tail. Slice the leek thinly, then fry with the butter for about 5 minutes in a large saucepan.

Add the stock, potatoes and seasoning. Bring to the boil, then simmer for 25 minutes. Remove from the heat, then liquidise. Before serving reheat the soup and stir in the cream.

Tomato Soup

Still one of the most popular soups. Why not try spicing it up by adding a few pinches of chilli powder? Great for those cold, dark nights when you're dressed in the latest blanket fashions and wondering if hot summers really ever existed or if you merely dreamt them up after reading a science fiction novel.

Serves 4

Ingredients

1 lb (500g) of tomatoes
1 onion, peeled and finely chopped
1 clove of garlic, peeled and chopped
1 bouquet garni
1 pint (600ml) of water
½ pint (300ml) of milk
1 tbs of oil
Salt
Pepper

Boil some water in a saucepan, then place the tomatoes in it. Remove the pan from the heat and leave for about 5 minutes. Take the tomatoes from the water and peel off the skins. Chop into small pieces.

Fry the tomatoes, garlic and onions gently in the oil for about 15 minutes until they go mushy. Add the water and bouquet garni, then simmer for 1 hour. If you don't want bits in your soup you can sieve it. Otherwise, just add the milk to the tomato mixture and stir. Season. Simmer for about 3 minutes, then serve.

Vegetable Soup

At the end of the summer there is usually an abundance of fresh vegetables available from local nurseries. I buy vast quantities of tomatoes and make up batches of tomato sauce and soup that can be frozen and used when needed during the winter, but that's because I've got nothing better to do. There are no limits as to what vegetables you can use. This is just a guideline.

Serves 4

Ingredients

2 tbs of oil
1 onion, peeled and chopped
1 leek, thinly sliced
2 cabbage leaves, shredded or finely chopped
1 courgette, finely chopped
1 carrot, scraped and sliced
1 tsp mixed herbs
1 bay leaf
2 pints (1 litre) of vegetable stock
Salt
Pepper

Heat the oil in a large saucepan, then fry the onions for about 5 minutes or until they have softened. Then add the other vegetables and fry for a further 10 minutes. Add the stock and herbs then season. Bring to the boil, then simmer for 30 minutes. Remove the bay leaf before serving. If you want a smoother texture, liquidise the soup before serving.

Gazpacho

This is a thin chilled soup that is very refreshing on a hot summer's evening. A blender is needed for this recipe. I often add a dash of tabasco sauce, but this is optional.

Serves 4

Ingredients

8 oz (225g) ripe tomatoes, skinned
½ green pepper, deseeded and chopped
½ red pepper, deseeded and chopped
½ cucumber
1 pint (600ml) of tomato juice
1 onion, peeled and chopped
1 clove of garlic, peeled and chopped
2 tbs of olive oil
1 tbs tarragon vinegar
1 tbs of fresh chives
1 tbs of fresh parsley
Salt
Pepper

Chop all the vegetables into chunks and put aside a little of each for the garnish. Place all the ingredients except for the oil into a blender for 2 minutes or so. Then add the oil and seasoning, place in the fridge for at least 3 hours. A few ice cubes can be added to speed up this process, but don't add too many as it will make the soup weak. Serve with the reserved vegetables (not the extrovert ones).

Chilled Cucumber Soup

This is another soup that is ideal for serving during the summer months, or weeks if you live in Britain.

Serves 4

Ingredients

2 cucumbers, peeled and sliced
1 tbs of flour
½ pint (300ml) of water
½ tsp of grated nutmeg
¼ pint (150ml) of single cream
1 bay leaf
1 tbs fresh mint, chopped
Salt
Pepper

Place the cucumber into a saucepan with the water and cook until tender. Remove from the heat and then put in a blender for a minute or so, until smooth. Return the cucumber to the saucepan and stir in the flour. Add the seasoning and bayleaf, then slowly bring to the boil. Simmer for 5 minutes then cool and strain. Once strained stir in the cream and chill in the fridge for a couple of hours. Before serving decorate with the mint.

Curried Parsnip and Apple Soup

A liquidiser is required for this recipe.

Serves 4

Ingredients

2 tbs of oil
1 large onion, peeled and chopped
1 ½ lb (750g) parsnips, peeled and chopped
1 apple, peeled and cored
2 tsp medium curry powder
2 pints (1 litre) of vegetable stock
Salt
Pepper

Heat the oil in a large saucepan, then fry the onions and curry powder for about 5 minutes until they have softened. Add the apple and the parsnips and fry gently for another 5 minutes. Add the stock and bring to the boil, then simmer for 30 minutes. Transfer the soup into a liquidiser and blend until smooth.

Serve with fresh crusty bread. If you don't like the flavour of curry then omit the powder.

Pumpkin Soup

This recipe requires a liquidiser.

Serves 4

Ingredients

1 ½ lb (750g) of pumpkin flesh, cut into cubes
½ pint (300ml) of milk
4 oz (100g) of butter
Salt
Pepper

Melt the butter in a saucepan, then fry the pumpkin until it is soft and mushy. Season, then add milk and put into a liquidiser for a minute. Put the liquid back into a saucepan and heat through, but do not boil.

Salads

Thankfully the days are long gone when a salad consisted only of a limp lettuce leaf, a tomato and a few crinkled slices of cucumber. There is an increasingly exotic selection of salad vegetables available: some supermarkets stock up to ten different varieties of lettuce alone. Salads are still more popular during the summer months when the produce is cheaper.

Potato Salad

This recipe can be made with either salad cream or mayonnaise, according to taste. Chopped fresh chives can be added if required.

Serves 4

Ingredients

5 medium-sized potatoes
Mayonnaise
Salt
Pepper

If you are using new potatoes the skins can be left on, just scrub them. Place the potatoes in boiling water for 15 minutes or until a knife will pass through the centre fairly easily. After the potatoes have cooled, cut into halves or quarters depending on the size, place in a bowl and dollop some mayonnaise on top. Mix together and season.

Chopped fresh chives can be added if you like. If you are using small new potatoes they can be left whole. Another alternative to using mayonnaise is to place new potatoes in bowl with a couple of tablespoons of olive oil or melted butter.

Cucumber Salad

Cucumbers are very high in water content and provide little nutritional benefit, but they are refreshing to eat.

Serves 4

Ingredients

1 large cucumber
1 tbs white wine vinegar
1 tsp sugar
1 tbs olive oil
2 tbs chopped fresh chives
Salt
Pepper

Peel the cucumber and slice as thinly as possible. A mandolin is ideal for producing wafer thin slices. Arrange the slices of cucumber on a flat plate and sprinkle generously with salt. Place another plate of a similar size on top and press down gently. Leave in the fridge for 1 hour. Remove from the fridge and pour away the water that has been extracted. Mix the vinegar, oil and sugar together, then pour over the cucumber. Season, then sprinkle the chopped chives on top.

Tomato and Feta Salad

Serves 4

Ingredients

6 ripe tomatoes
4 oz (100g) feta cheese
10 black olives
Olive oil
Salt
Pepper

Slice the tomatoes and arrange on flat plate or platter dish. Cut the cheese into cubes or crumble into small pieces and place on top of the tomatoes. Arrange the olives on top, season, then drizzle with oil.

The Big Salad

This is the only way to describe this salad, think of it as more of a meal than just as a salad.

Serves 4

Ingredients

1 cos lettuce
1 avocado
4 tomatoes
4 medium-sized new potatoes
4 eggs
4 thin slices of French bread
1 clove of garlic
1 tbs hazlenuts
French Dressing
Salt
Pepper

Scrub or peel the potatoes, then cut in half. Cook in salted boiling water for 15 minutes or so. Whilst the potatoes are cooking prepare the salad stuff. Wash the lettuce and tomatoes, then cut the tomatoes into quarters. Remove the skin of the avocado and cut in two. Ease out the stone and discard. Chop the avocado into cubes and sprinkle over a little lemon juice.

Lightly toast the French bread on both sides. Peel the garlic and cut in two. Rub the garlic over the toast and then drizzle with olive oil. Place the salad ingredients, nuts, avocado and toast in a large serving bowl and stir in 6 tbs of French dressing.

Now poach the eggs. If you get caught by the farmer, there

are two other ways of doing it: you can either use an egg poacher, or if you do not possess such an implement you can boil some water in a large saucepan then just gently break the eggs into the water. Cook the eggs for 3-5 minutes depending on taste. In this recipe it is nice if the yolk is runny but the white is cooked.

When the eggs are cooked remove from the water and place on top of the salad.

Avocado and Cottage Cheese Salad

Serves 2

Ingredients

2 ripe avocado pears
8 oz (225g) cottage cheese
10 green seedless grapes
1 tbs walnuts
2 oz (50g) mushrooms
4 tbs of French dressing

Wipe and slice the mushrooms. Peel the avocados then remove the stone. Cut the avocado into chunks, place in a serving bowl then pour over the dressing. Chop the grapes in half and add to the serving bowl along with the cheese, walnuts and the mushrooms.

Spinach and Pine Nut Salad

Only use young spinach leaves in this salad — don't even contemplate using frozen spinach or seaweed.

Serves 4

Ingredients

1 lb (500g) spinach
4 oz (100g) celery
1 red pepper, cored and deseeded
2 oz (50g) pine nuts
1 tbs cashew nuts
1 tbs sultanas
5 tbs French dressing
Salt
Pepper

Make sure there are no tough stalks on the spinach then wash and drain. Rinse the celery then chop into bite-sized pieces. Having cut the pepper into thin strips chuck all the ingredients together in a serving bowl, season and mix well.

Coleslaw

Delicious with salads, it also provides a handy stand-by if you need to pebble-dash a small area of wall.

Serves 4

Ingredients

8 oz (225g) of white cabbage, grated
2 carrots, scraped and grated
1 small onion, peeled and grated
5 to 6 tbs of mayonnaise
Salt
Pepper

If you have time, soak the cabbage for an hour to make it crisp. If not, it doesn't really matter. After soaking the cabbage, dry with a kitchen towel and put in a large serving bowl with the carrots and onion. Stir in the mayonnaise, and season.

There are many variations of this recipe. Additional ingredients can include chopped apple, sultanas, and nuts.

Tabbouleh

Bulghur wheat is made from wheat that has been boiled, dried, then ground. As an ingredient it is widely used in countries like Morocco and Tunisia. Tabbouleh is a perfect dish for serving at a buffet supper, it makes an interesting contrast to traditional salads.

Serves 4

Ingredients

6 oz (150g) of bulghur wheat
4 tbs of olive oil
½ cucumber, chopped
2 tomatoes, peeled and chopped
1 bunch of spring onions
1 bunch of parsley
8 mint leaves, chopped
Juice of one lemon
Salt
Pepper

Place the bulghur wheat in a saucepan of water. Bring to the boil, then simmer gently for 10 to 15 minutes until tender. Drain, then allow to cool.

Finely chop the parsley and the spring onions. Place the bulghur in a serving bowl, add the olive oil, parsley, mint, tomato, cucumber, spring onions, lemon juice, salt and pepper. Mix together thoroughly.

Vegetable Side Dishes

Side dishes are an essential part of every mealtime: how else would you get those mysterious stains on your elbows? Here are some particularly messy varieties.

French Beans with Garlic

If you have trouble communicating with French beans because your French is a little rusty, you could use runner beans instead.

Serves 4

Ingredients

1 lb (500g) French beans
1 clove of garlic, peeled and finely chopped
1 oz (25g) butter
Salt
Pepper

Top and tail the beans then cut in two. Place the beans in a pan of salted boiling water and cook for 10 minutes or until tender. It is important that they are not over-cooked as they will lose their colour and flavour. When cooked, drain the beans. Heat the butter in the pan and let it melt, but don't let it burn. Add the garlic and cook for a minute then add the beans and season. Stir the beans to make sure they are evenly coated before serving.

Courgettes can be cooked in a similar way, except they don't need to be boiled – they can be fried gently in the butter with the garlic.

Okra and Tomatoes

Okra are also referred to ladies' fingers *which whilst not necessarily whetting the appetite is a mite better than* ladies' toes.

Serves 4

Ingredients

3 tbs olive oil
1 lb (500g) okra
1 lb (500g) tomatoes
1 small onion, peeled and chopped
1 clove of garlic, peeled and crushed
1 tbs lemon juice
1 tsp garam masala
2 tbs chopped coriander
Salt
Pepper

Trim the thick ends of the okra and then cut them in half. Place the tomatoes in boiling water for 1 minute. Remove the tomato skins and quarter.

Heat the oil in a large frying pan, then cook the onion for 5 minutes. Add the okra and cook for a further 5 minutes. Stir in the other ingredients, except for the coriander and cook until the okra is tender. Garnish with the coriander.

Dauphinoise Potatoes

If I could only eat potatoes cooked one way it would have to be this. The combination of potatoes and cream is delicious. They go particularly well with dishes such as hot vegetable stew.

Serves 4

Ingredients

2 lb (1kg) 'old' potatoes, peeled and thinly sliced
1 large onion, peeled and thinly sliced
2 cloves of garlic, peeled and crushed
½ pint (300ml) double cream
2 oz (50g) butter
Nutmeg
Salt
Pepper

Grease the base and sides of an ovenproof dish, then put alternate layers of onion, potato, garlic, slices of butter, cream, salt, pepper and grated nutmeg in the dish. Finish with a layer of potatoes. Place in a preheated oven at Gas Mark 5 (400 °F, 200 °C) for about 1 + hours. If required, freshly grated cheese such as gruyere or parmesan can be added.

N.B. Only a small amount of nutmeg is used on each layer because the flavour must not be overpowering.

Aubergine and Tofu Fritters

Serves 4

Ingredients

Vegetable oil
1 aubergine
1 small onion, peeled and finely chopped
4 oz (100g) tofu
2 tbs flour
1 tbs chopped parsley
Salt
Pepper

Peel the aubergine, then chop into small chunks. Place the aubergine in a mixing bowl and sprinkle liberally with salt and leave for 20 minutes. Then rinse and pat dry with kitchen paper. Mix in the tofu, onion, parsley and seasoning.

Heat the oil in a frying pan. The oil needs to be quite deep as the fritters have to be deep fried. When the oil is beginning to smoke, using a spoon take some of the mixture and mould it into something that resembles a fritter. Gently place a couple of the fritters at a time in the oil and fry until golden. When cooked drain on more kitchen paper to absorb the oil. Eat while still hot.

Spicy Potatoes

Serves 4

Ingredients

1 lb (500g) potatoes
Half a cup of water
3 tbs vegetable oil
¾-inch (2cm) cube of fresh ginger
2 fresh green chilli peppers
1 tsp mustard seeds
½ tsp tumeric

Cook the potatoes in boiling water for 10 minutes then drain. Peel when they are cool enough to handle. Heat the oil in a large saucepan or wok then add the mustard seeds. When the mustard seeds begin to pop, add the ginger, tumeric, chilli peppers, garam masala and cook for a minute.

Add the potatoes and the water the cook for a few minutes before serving.

Grilled Courgettes with Parmesan

This is not really a main dish, but more of a starter or side dish.

Serves 2

Ingredients

4 courgettes
4 tbs olive oil
2 oz (50g) parmesan, finely grated
1 clove of garlic, peeled and finely chopped
Salt
Pepper

Heat the grill to its highest setting. Cut the courgettes into diagonal slices about 2 cm thick. Mix together the oil, garlic, pepper and salt. Brush each side of the courgettes with the oil then grill for 3 minutes on each side. Then sprinkle the cheese on top of the courgettes and grill until the cheese melts.

Serve immediately with warm bread.

Pizza

This genre of food offers enormous variety to vegetarians — it's always possible to have a *pizza what you fancy*. Pizzas are pretty easy to make, quick to cook, and very filling.

Pizza Dough

If you don't have the time to make your own dough then you can slum it and buy ready-made bases. If you don't have time to buy ready-made bases, try getting up earlier in the day.

Serves 4

Ingredients

1 lb (500g) sifted plain flour
1 tsp sugar
250 ml (8 fl oz) warm water
1 oz (25g) fresh yeast
Pinch of salt
3 tbs olive oil

Having sifted the flour into a bowl add a pinch of salt. Dissolve the yeast in half of the water then add the sugar. The sugar is used to activate the yeast which after 10 minutes should have begun to froth. When it gets to this stage add the flour, oil and a little water so a firm paste is produced. Stir in the remaining water and knead the mixture until you form a smooth stretchy dough. Place a damp tea towel over the top of the bowl and leave in a warm place for about 45 minutes.

After 45 minutes the dough should have doubled in size. Knead for a couple of minutes then cover and leave to rest for about 20-30 minutes.

Divide the dough into four equal portions then roll them out on a lightly floured board or clean work-surface. They should be about half a centimetre in thickness and preferably round. Use your hand to help manipulate the dough.

While you are messing about with the dough, stick the oven on full blast.

When you have the dough to the desired shape, add your favourite topping, then cook for 20 minutes or until cooked. Make sure that you don't make the base too thick otherwise it will go soggy.

Garlic Pizza

If you have made your own dough, then try this!

Serves 1

Ingredients

1 portion of pizza dough
6 tbs olive oil
1 clove of garlic, peeled and finely chopped

Mix the oil and garlic together. Take a quarter of the dough and it roll out as thin as you can get it without it tearing. Cover the surface lightly with the garlic oil and bake until golden. You can experiment by changing the thickness of the base or by adding more or less garlic.

Pizza Margherita

This is where dough becomes real pizza. If you want to design your own, begin with this and add your own toppings.

Serves 1

Ingredients

1 pizza base
2 tinned tomatoes, chopped
1 tsp of olive oil
2 oz (50g) of cubed mozzarella
Pinch of oregano
Salt
Pepper

Spread the chopped tomatoes on top of the pizza base. A thin layer will do — if you put too much on your pizza will become soggy. Place the cheese on top, season, add the herbs and pour on the oil. Bake in the oven until the cheese turns a golden brown colour. It should take roughly 20 minutes on the highest setting of your oven.

Pizza Dolce Vita

Serves 1

Ingredients

1 pizza base
2 tinned tomatoes, chopped
1 tsp olive oil
2 oz (50g) cubed mozzarella
2 oz (50g) sliced mushrooms
Pinch of oregano
Salt
Pepper

Spread the chopped tomatoes on top of the pizza base then cover liberally with the mushrooms. Add the cheese then season and finally drizzle lightly with the oil. Place in a hot oven on its highest setting for about 20 minutes.

Pizza Pavarotti

Serves 1

Ingredients

1 pizza base
2 tinned tomatoes, chopped
1 tsp olive oil
2 oz (50g) cubed mozzarella
1 oz (25g) sliced mushrooms
3 slices of onion

2 slices of red pepper
1 egg
4 olives
Pinch of oregano
Salt
Pepper

Spread the chopped tomatoes on top of the pizza base then cover liberally with the mushrooms, onion, pepper and olives.. Add the cheese then break the egg on top, season and finally drizzle lightly with the oil. Place in a hot oven on its highest setting for about 20 minutes.

Pizza Don Giovanni

Serves 1

Ingredients

1 pizza base
2 tinned tomatoes, chopped
1 tsp olive oil
2 oz (50g) cubed mozzarella
5 spinach leaves
1 oz (25g) pine nuts
Salt
Pepper

Spread the chopped tomatoes on top of the pizza base then add the spinach leaves. Add the cheese and pine nuts then season and finally drizzle lightly with the oil. Place in a hot oven on its highest setting for about 20 minutes.

Main Meals

Cauliflower and Courgette Casserole

Serves 4

Ingredients

1 cauliflower, cut in florets
1 courgette, sliced
2 tbs of olive oil
1 onion, peeled and roughly chopped
2 cloves of garlic, peeled and finely chopped
1 tin of chopped tomatoes
1 tbs of chopped fresh ginger
1 tsp of chilli powder
2 tbs of chopped fresh parsley
1 pinch of dried nutmeg
4 tbs breadcrumbs
6 oz (150g) grated cheddar cheese
Salt
Pepper

Preheat the oven to Gas Mark 6, 425 °F, 220 °C.

Heat the oil in a large saucepan and fry the onions for a couple of minutes. Add the courgette, garlic, herbs, spices and seasoning then gently cook for another 5 minutes. Whilst these are cooking, boil a pan of water and cook the cauliflower for 5 minutes. Cauliflower is one of those vegetables that is most unforgiving about being over-cooked, so time it carefully unless you are prepared to eat a stodgy mess.

When the cauliflower is cooked to perfection, drain and add to the onions. Stir in the tomatoes and transfer it all to a casserole dish. Mix the breadcrumbs and cheese together and sprinkle of top.

Place in the oven for 25 minutes. Serve with brown rice.

Mushroom Risotto

Serves 4

Ingredients

4 oz (100g) mushrooms
8 oz (250g) rice
1 onion, peeled and finely chopped
1 red pepper, cored and chopped
1 tsp dried thyme
1 tbs of chopped fresh parsley
2 oz (50g) butter
2 pints of vegetable stock
Salt
Pepper

Melt the butter in a large saucepan or frying pan. Fry the onion for 3 minutes then add the pepper and mushrooms and continue frying for another 5 minutes. Stir in the rice then add the vegetable stock and bring to the boil. Chuck in the herbs and season then simmer for about 20 minutes. It is important that you make sure that the pan does not boil dry. If it is getting a little dry add a few spoons of water.

Cheese and Tomato Flan

Serves 4

Ingredients

8 oz (200g) short crust pastry
3 eggs
6 tomatoes
4 oz (100g) grated cheddar cheese
¼ pint (150ml) milk
Oregano
Salt
Pepper

Preheat the oven to Gas Mark 6, 425 °F, 220 °C.

If you are using ready-made pastry make sure it is has totally defrosted. Roll out the pastry so that it can cover a medium-sized flan dish. Place the rolled out pastry in the dish and using a fork prick holes all over. Bake for about 5 minutes, then allow to cool.

While the flan is cooking place the tomatoes in a pan of boiling water for a couple of minutes. Remove and drain. When they are cool enough to handle take off their skins and slice thinly.

Beat the eggs together, mix in the cheese and season. Place the sliced tomatoes on the base of the flan and cover with the egg and cheese mixture. Sprinkle with a little oregano, then bake for 30-40 minutes.

Soya Bean Stew

Before using soya beans they must be soaked overnight, then cooked for three hours, and shouted at for twenty minutes.

Serves 4

Ingredients

8 oz (225g) soya beans
2 tbs oil
1 onion, peeled and finely chopped
1 clove of garlic, peeled and finely chopped
14 oz tin of chopped tomatoes
4 oz (100g) mushrooms
1 tbs tomato purée
3 tsp of paprika
2 pints (1 litre) of water
4 tbs chopped parsley
Salt
Pepper

Preheat the oven to Gas Mark 4, 350 °F, 180 °C.
Drain the beans after they have been soaked and cooked.

Heat the oil in a frying pan then cook the onions garlic for a couple of minutes. Transfer the contents of the frying pan into a large casserole dish then add the remaining ingredients and season according to taste. Put the lid on the casserole and place in the oven and cook for 90 minutes.

Aduki Beans with Wild Rice

First catch your wild rice . . .

Serves 4

Ingredients

8 oz (225g) aduki beans
6 oz (150g) wild rice
2 tbs oil
1 onion, peeled and chopped
2 cloves of garlic, peeled and finely chopped
1 tbs chopped fresh parsley
1 tsp chilli powder
14 oz tin of chopped tomatoes
1 tbs tomato purée
1 pint (500ml) bitter
Salt
Pepper

Soak the beans overnight, then drain and rinse.

Heat the oil in a large saucepan. Gently fry the onion for 5 minutes then add the garlic and continue cooking for another 2 minutes. Stir in the rice and cook for about a minute. Then add the beans, tomatoes, purée, chilli, parsley, beer and seasoning. Bring to the boil, then reduce to a gentle simmer, keeping a lid on the pan.

Cook for 40 minutes then serve with sliced courgettes.

Spinach Curry

If your local spinach shop is low on stock, seaweed makes a revolting substitute if you live near the sea.

Serves 4

Ingredients

3 tbs oil
2 lb (1000g) spinach
1 large onion, peeled and chopped
2 cloves of garlic, peeled and finely chopped
1 red pepper, deseeded
3 tomatoes, quartered
2 tsp tomato purée
1 tbs madras curry powder

Remove any tough stems from the spinach then wash. Place the washed spinach in a deep saucepan (no need to add any water) and cook gently for 10 minutes. Whilst the spinach is cooking, heat the oil in a large frying pan then cook the onions for 5 minutes, being careful not to let them brown. Then add the peppers and garlic and cook for about 5 minutes. Next in is curry powder, shortly followed by the tomatoes and tomato purée. Continue cooking for another 5 minutes.

When the spinach is cooked drain thoroughly so there is no liquid left, then chop roughly. Finally add the spinach to the frying pan and heat through.

Cheese Fondu

A favourite of the Swiss. Basically melted cheese in which you dunk pieces of bread. Try buying a number of different breads, such as walnut, olive bread, or a simple white sliced loaf.

Serves 4

Ingredients

1 oz (25g) butter
1 oz (25g) flour
5 fl oz (150ml) milk
2 egg yolks
5 fl oz (150g) single cream
10 oz grated gruyère cheese
Salt
Pepper

Melt the butter in a medium-sized saucepan then stir in the flour until a soft paste is formed. Add the milk slowly, stirring constantly with a wooden spoon so no lumps are formed. When all the milk has been added, pour in the cream and cheese, then season.

Heat gently until the cheese has melted then remove from the heat. Beat in the egg yolks and serve immediately.

If you have a food warmer keep the saucepan on top of this as this will keep the cheese warm and runny.

Eggs Florentine

If your budget can stretch to it use parmesan instead of the cheddar.

Serves 4

Ingredients

2 lb (1000g) fresh spinach
4 eggs
3 oz (75g) grated cheddar or parmesan
6 tbs double cream
1 tbs pine nuts
Pinch of grated nutmeg
Salt
Pepper

Preheat the oven to Gas Mark 6 225 °C 425 °F

Rinse the spinach then drain into a colander. Put the spinach in a saucepan then cook gently for 6 minutes without adding any water. When cooked remove from the pan and drain any remaining juice, then chop finely.

Return the spinach back to the pan and stir in the cream, nutmeg, salt, pepper and pinenuts, heating gently through for a minute or two. Lightly grease an ovenproof dish then make four 'birds' nests' using the spinach. Break the eggs gently into the nests and sprinkle with cheese.

Place the dish in the preheated oven for 10-15 minutes depending on how you like your eggs.

Beef Tomatoes Stuffed with Vermicelli

Don't panic, there's not even a hint of mad cow in this recipe. Beef tomatoes are those particularly large ones and are ideal for stuffing.

Serves 4

Ingredients

4 large beef tomatoes
4 oz (100g) vermicelli
1 clove of garlic, peeled and finely chopped
1 tbs of capers
1 tsp oregano
1 tbs fresh parsley
Salt
Pepper

Wash the tomatoes then cut the tops off, keeping them by as they are needed as lids. With a large spoon scoop out all the flesh from the tomato, being careful not to damage the skin. Do not throw the flesh away as it is needed later.

Put the vermicelli into a plastic bag and lightly crush, then cook in boiling water until it is almost cooked. Drain, then add the oil, garlic, capers, herbs, salt, pepper and finally two tablespoons of the tomato flesh. Mix all the ingredients together, then place the mixture back in the tomatoes.

Place the stuffed tomatoes in a lightly oiled baking dish then cook for about 30 minutes on Gas Mark 3, 160 °C, 325 °F.

Crunchy Rice

Serves 2 to 4

Ingredients

2 tbs of oil
2 cups of wholemeal rice
4 cups of water
1 green pepper, deseeded and chopped
1 small tin of sweetcorn
1 onion, peeled and chopped
1 oz (25g) of mushrooms, sliced
1 clove of garlic, peeled and finely chopped
2 oz (50g) of walnuts
1 vegetarian stock cube
1 tbs fresh chopped parsley
Salt
Pepper

Heat the oil in a large frying pan or wok, then fry the onions and garlic for between 4 and 5 minutes. Add the mushrooms, green pepper and sweetcorn and fry for another couple of minutes. Next add the uncooked rice and about four cups of water. Sprinkle the stock cube over and stir frequently. Simmer for about 20 minutes, depending on the type of rice used. Add more water if necessary to stop the rice from drying out.

If the rice is soft when pinched then it is cooked. Add the walnuts a couple of minutes before removing from the heat. Season with salt and pepper and garnish with the parsley.

Piperade

This is one of those dishes that is quick and easy to prepare and is suitable for a light lunch or supper. The dish originates from the Basque country, close to the paella factory. If you want it with a little bite, add some paprika (or some shark's teeth).

Serves 4

Ingredients

6 eggs
2 tbs butter
2 red peppers, deseeded
2 green peppers, deseeded
2 cloves of garlic, peeled and chopped
6 tomatoes, skinned
1 tbs chopped fresh basil
Salt
Pepper

Cut the peppers into strips and chop the tomatoes. Heat the butter in a frying pan and cook the peppers for 10 minutes. Add the chopped tomatoes, garlic, basil and seasoning and cook until the tomatoes are almost to a pulp. Take care that the vegetables do not burn.

Whilst the vegetables are cooking, beat the eggs in a basin. When the vegetables are ready add the eggs. Stir the mixture until it thickens, but do not let the eggs set completely.

Wholewheat Pancakes

These pancakes are ideal for serving with ratatouille.

Serves 4

Ingredients

¾ pint (400ml) milk
6 oz (150g) wholewheat flour
1 egg, beaten
2 tsp butter
Salt

Put the flour in a mixing bowl and add a pinch of salt. Make a well in the centre of the flour then drop in the egg. Using a wooden spoon gradually combine the egg and the flour until a smooth paste is formed. Gradually add the milk making sure no lumps are formed. Melt the butter and allow to cool for a minute, then add to the mixture. The addition of the butter helps to stop them from sticking to the bottom of the pan.

When making pancakes it is always advisable to leave the mixture for at least 30 minutes before cooking.

Vegetable Chilli

You can add a meat substitue such as quorn or tofu for this recipe but it tastes equally good without.

Serves 4

Ingredients

2 tbs olive oil
1 onion, peeled and chopped
2 cloves of garlic, peeled and chopped
1 courgette, sliced
1 leek, thinly sliced
1 red pepper, de-seeded
2 carrots, chopped
1 tin of chopped tomatoes
1 tin of kidney beans
1 tbs tomato purée
2 tsp chilli powder
Salt
Pepper

Heat the oil in a large saucepan and fry the onion for about 5 minutes, making sure they do not burn. Then add the garlic and chilli powder and fry gently for a couple of minutes. Add the other vegetables and fry for a further five minutes. Stir in the remaining ingredients and season. Bring to the boil, then simmer for 40 minutes.

Serve with rice or a jacket potato.

Jacket Potato

Ingredients

I large old potato

After viciously stabbing your potato with a sharp implement (preferably a fork), bung in the oven for about 60 minutes on Gas Mark 7 (450 °F, 230 °C).

Test the potato with a skewer or a knife to see if it is cooked in the middle. The skewer should pass easily through the potato. For added crispiness, baste with oil and sprinkle a little salt on to the skin before putting in the oven.

Jacket Potato with Cheese and Onion

This is another way of cooking jacket potatoes, but it takes a little more time.

Ingredients

I large potato
2 oz (50g) of cheddar cheese, grated
I onion
I tbs of milk
A nob of butter

Follow the instructions for the above recipe. Slice the cooked potato in half. Scoop the potato out of the skin using a teaspoon and place the contents into a mixing bowl. Try not to make a hole in the skins because you'll need them later.

Add a tablespoon of milk and a nob of butter and mash. Cut the onion up into pieces and fry for 3 to 4 minutes. Add the onion to the potato and mix together. Then spoon the potato back into the jackets, cover with cheese and cook for another 15 minutes or so. If the cheese starts to burn cover the potato with a piece of tinfoil.

Macaroni Cheese

This is another of my favourite recipes. If you don't have any macaroni use pasta shells. If you don't have any pasta shells, use macaroni.

Serves 4

Ingredients

6 oz (150g) of macaroni
6 oz (150g) of grated cheddar cheese
2 large tomatoes
¾ pint (350ml) of milk
1 oz (25g) of flour or cornflour
1 oz (25g) of butter

Melt the butter in a saucepan and mix in the flour. Gradually add the milk, stirring constantly to prevent lumps. Bring to the boil, add the cheese, then leave to simmer for 3 to 4 minutes.

Now cook the macaroni according to the instructions on the packet. When this is done, drain and mix with the cheese sauce. Put into a baking dish, top with sliced tomatoes and more cheese. Grill until browned.

Vegetable Bake

Serves 4

Ingredients

2 tbs of oil
1 onion, peeled
1 clove of garlic
1 courgette
1 small tin of sweetcorn
1 tin of chopped tomatoes
1 oz (25g) of mushrooms
2 oz (50g) of cheddar
2 slices of bread
1 vegetarian stock cube
Mixed herbs
A slosh of red wine
Salt
Pepper

Preheat the oven to 150 °C (300 °F, Gas Mark 2). Slice the onion, garlic, courgette and mushrooms, and lightly fry in the oil for 5 minutes. Add the sweetcorn, tomatoes, herbs, seasoning and wine. Mix the stock cube with a cup of water and add to the pan, simmer for about 10 minutes.

If there is a food processor around, use it to turn the bread into breadcrumbs. Otherwise just tear the bread into small pieces with your bare (but clean) hands. Grate the cheese.

Pour the vegetables into a casserole dish and cover with breadcrumbs and cheese. Put into the oven for 10 to 20 minutes – until the breadcrumbs have gone crispy and the cheese has melted.

Alternatively, serve with cheese instead of breadcrumbs as a sauce for pasta or rice.

Cabbage Parcels

Don't forget to affix sufficient postage.

Serves 2

Ingredients

6 large cabbage leaves
8 oz (225g) of spinach
6 oz (150g) of cooked rice
2 oz (50g) of butter
4 oz (100g) of grated cheddar cheese
1 egg yolk
½ pint (300ml) of vegetable stock

First, simmer the spinach in a little water for 5 minutes, then drain and put aside. Simmer the cabbage leaves for about two minutes and remove from the water. Melt the butter and add the chopped onion together with the rice, spinach, cheese, and seasoning. Bind with the egg yolk.

When thoroughly mixed, put a heaped spoonful of it onto each of the cabbage leaves, and wrap into parcels. Place the parcels in an ovenproof dish and pour the stock on top. Cover with foil and bake for 30 minutes at Gas Mark 4, 350 °F, 180 °C.

Potato and Tomato Cakes

This is based on an Italian dish that is delicious served hot or cold.

Serves 4

Ingredients

2 tbs of oil
2 lb (1 kg) of 'old' potatoes
1 tin of chopped tomatoes
1 onion, peeled and finely chopped
Salt
Pepper

Heat the oil in a pan and fry the onion gently for 10 minutes then add the tomato, salt and pepper. Keep the heat low and simmer for about 20 minutes so the sauce reduces to a thick liquid. Whilst the sauce is reducing boil the potatoes until they are soft enough to mash. When they get to this stage mash them. Gradually mix the sauce with the mashed potatoes. When all the sauce is added, spoon the mixture out onto a serving plate and mould into the shape of a cake or an amusingly clever 'naughty' shape.

Bubble and Squeak

This requires scraping the leftovers from the previous day/week out of the bin-liner, then melting it down to a substance slightly less chewy than industrial glue.

Ingredients

2 tbs of oil
Mashed potato
Greens or brussels sprouts
Egg
Whatever else has got stuck to the saucepan overnight

Kill any ingredients that are still moving. Fry the mixture until it smells edible, then eat if you dare. This meal may reproduce itself day after day.

Quiche

For this recipe an 8-inch (20 cm) flan dish and a rolling pin are needed.

Once the basic technique of making a quiche is mastered, limitless combinations of this classic French dish can be produced. Many people are put off preparing a quiche because it involves making pastry, but it's actually easier than you might think.

Short Crust Pastry

Ingredients for pastry

8 oz (225g) of plain flour
4 oz (100g) of margarine/butter
3 tbs of water
A pinch of salt

After sieving the flour and the salt add the butter. The fat is easier to rub in if it is cut into little cubes. The term 'rubbing in' is the procedure in which, using the fingertips, the flour and the fat are combined to produce a consistency of fine bread crumbs.

After rubbing in, add some water a little at a time. The water is needed to bind the mixture together, but be careful not to add so much that the pastry becomes sticky. Mould the pastry into a ball then roll out on a floured board or a very clean floured work surface. Also sprinkle a coating of flour onto the rolling pin. The flour is used to stop the pastry from sticking to the board and the pin.

Roll the pastry so that its area is big enough to cover the flan dish, then carefully place the pastry over the dish and mould it in the shape of the dish. Remove the edge of the overlapping pastry by running a knife along the rim of dish.

The next stage is to make the filling of the quiche.
An important point to remember is that before adding the filling to the pastry case, the pastry should be 'baked blind'. This does not involve putting on a blindfold and trying to find the oven – baking blind is where a pastry case is pre-cooked in the oven for about 15 minutes. The pastry case has to be lined with dried lentils or dried peas (in order to stop the pastry from rising). If the pastry case is not baked blind there is a good chance that it will be soggy.

Cheese and Onion Quiche

Ingredients for filling

1 tbs of oil
4 eggs
½ pint (300ml) of milk
4 oz (100g) of grated cheddar cheese
1 onion, peeled and chopped
Salt
Pepper

Lightly fry the onions in the oil for a couple of minutes. Place the onion on the bottom of the pastry case. Beat the eggs together, add the milk, season and beat again. Pour over the onion, sprinkle the cheese on top, then bake in a hot oven on Gas Mark 6 (425 °F, 220 °C), for 25 minutes or until the filling is cooked. Serve with a smile.

Vegetable Stir-fry

Those fortunate enough to possess a wok will find Oriental cooking a lot easier than those stuck with the indignity of a frying pan. If you do have to use a frying pan, use the biggest one you have. The wok is one of my most used kitchen accessories – its use does not have to be confined to Oriental cooking.

It's up to you what to put into a stir-fry, though it is often a good way of using up any spare vegetables that are lurking at the back of your cupboard. Experiment with exotic vegetables, oils and pastes.

Serves 4

Ingredients

2 tbs of oil
1 onion, peeled and chopped
1 red pepper, deseeded and chopped
1 green pepper, deseeded and chopped
1 carrot, cut into thin strips
1 clove of garlic, peeled and finely chopped
1 tin of bamboo shoots
1 tin of water chestnuts
1 pack of fresh beansprouts
2 tbs of soy sauce
Salt
Pepper

Pour the oil into your wok, then when the oil is hot, i.e. when it is smoking (try not to set fire to the kitchen in the process), add the onion and garlic and fry for 5 minutes. If you are using water chestnuts, cook these first as they take the longest to cook, and are nicer when they are slightly crispy. Add the soy sauce, seasoning, and other vegetables except for the beansprouts.

After frying the vegetables for about 5 to 10 minutes finally add the beansprouts and cook for a couple more minutes. Serve with rice.

Lentil Curry

Serves 2

Ingredients

2 tbs oil
4 oz (100g) of lentils soaked in cold water for 1 hour
½ pint (300ml) of vegetable stock
4 carrots, scraped and chopped
1 onion, peeled and chopped
1 courgette, sliced
1 leek, sliced
1 tbs of curry powder
2 fresh tomatoes sliced
Salt
Pepper

Boil the lentils for about 7 minutes and then strain. Heat the oil in a large saucepan, then fry the onions and curry powder for 5 minutes. Add the other vegetables and fry for another 5 minutes. Then pour in the stock and lentils, bring to the boil, then simmer for an hour. Season.

Serve with rice.

Stuffed Marrow

It is possible to stuff a variety of vegetables. Naturally the bigger the vegetable the easier it is to stuff.

Serves 4

Ingredients

3 tbs of oil
1 large marrow
1 onion, peeled and chopped
8 oz (225g) of rice
1 tin of chopped tomatoes
3 oz (75g) of mushrooms, chopped
Bunch of parsley
1 tsp of mixed herbs
Salt
Pepper

Wash the marrow then cut a lengthways slice off the top. Using a large spoon remove the seeds. This should create a substantial hollow. Sprinkle the inside of the marrow with salt then turn it upside down.

Heat the oil in a large frying pan and fry the onion for about 5 minutes. Add the rice and cook for another couple of minutes. Now add the other ingredients except the marrow, adding a few tablespoons of water if needed. Cook for 15 minutes.

Rinse the marrow with water and then shake dry. Fill the marrow with the contents of the frying pan then replace the top and wrap in foil.

Bake on the middle shelf of the oven at Gas Mark 4 (350 °F,

180 °C) for about 80 minutes. It might take longer depending on the size of the marrow. Once a skewer can pass easily through the flesh of the marrow it is ready to be served.

Ratatouille

This traditional Provençal recipe can really be made from whatever vegetables are available. Tinned tomatoes are cheaper than buying fresh ones (except in the summer when fresh ones are more affordable).

The lemon is considered optional by some, but I believe it to be essential.

Serves 4

Ingredients

2 tbs of oil
1 tin of chopped tomatoes
1 onion, peeled and finely chopped
2 cloves of garlic, peeled and finely chopped
1 small aubergine, chopped
1 red pepper, deseeded and chopped
1 courgette, sliced
1 lemon, quartered
2 tsp of herbes de Provence
1 bay leaf
A glass of red wine, water or tomato juice (optional)
Pepper
Salt

While you are preparing the other vegetables, place the pieces of aubergine on a plate and sprinkle them with salt.

After preparing the other vegetables, wash the aubergine pieces then dry them with kitchen paper.

Heat the oil in a large saucepan. Fry the onions and garlic for about 5 minutes, then add the courgette, the aubergines and the peppers. Cook for about 5 minutes before adding the tomatoes, lemon, and other ingredients. Bring to the boil and simmer for 30 minutes.

Ratatouille can be served with almost anything – rice, baked potato, pitta bread etc. It can also be served cold.

N.B If you want a crisper tasting ratatouille then only cook the vegetables for about 10 minutes. More of the colours of the vegetables are retained as well.

Vegetable Curry

Trying to produce the perfect curry is not easy unless you have those authentic accompaniments such as a wall-to-wall mauve carpet, high-backed carpeted chairs, background Sitar music, steaming hot towels that enable one to have a quick wash at the end of the meal and the all-important local rugby team exposing themselves at the table next to you. It's enough to make you choke on your poppadom, but the food is great.

If you are interested in cooking Indian food then buy a book on the subject as I am not going to attempt to explain the complexities that are involved, such as grinding your own spices. For now I have included a basic curry that uses readily available ingredients and pre-ground curry powder.

Serves 4

Ingredients

2 tbs of oil
4 potatoes, diced into 1-inch (2.5cm) cubes
1 sliced leek
1 tin of chopped tomatoes
2 sliced courgettes
1 onion, peeled and chopped
2 cloves of garlic, peeled and finely chopped
1 small pot of natural yoghurt
1 tbs of Madras curry powder
1 dried red chilli
½ pint (300ml) of vegetable stock
Any spare vegetables
1 to 2 tbs of water

Heat the oil in a large saucepan then fry the onion, garlic and curry powder for 5 minutes or until they have softened. Add the other ingredients, except the yoghurt, bring to the boil, and simmer for 40 minutes or more. Stir in the yoghurt 5 minutes before serving.

Whilst the curry is simmering, taste it to see if it is to the strength required. If it is not hot enough for your asbestos-lined mouth just add more curry powder.

Serve with rice, preferably pilau or basmati.

Vegetable Kebabs

You do not have to stick to the vegetables suggested in this recipe.

Serves 2

Ingredients

1 oz (25g) of butter
1 green pepper, deseeded and cut into pieces
1 courgette, cut into chunks
1 small onion, peeled and quartered
2 tomatoes, quartered
4 mushrooms, halved or quartered
Salt
Pepper

Thread all the vegetables onto a couple of skewers and daub them with butter, then grill for about 15 minutes.

For a different flavour try adding a tablespoon of runny honey or a dash of soy sauce whilst grilling.

Serve with rice.

Leeks with Sesame Seeds

One of the more successful spin-offs from Sesame Street, *the hit television show for American undergraduates, the quantity of sesame seeds sold each year would make a pile bigger than one of Big Bird's whitish deposits.*

Serves 4

Ingredients

1 lb (500g) leeks
1 tbs olive oil
1 tsp French mustard
2 tbs white wine vinegar
4 tbs sesame seeds
Salt
Pepper

Preheat the oven to Gas Mark 6 (425 °F, 225 °C).

Trim the ends of the leeks then wash. Cut the leeks into 6 cm chunks then cook in boiling water for about 5 minutes. They must not be over-cooked as the leeks are going to be cooked in the oven later on.

While the leeks are cooking, mix the oil, vinegar and mustard together. When the leeks are ready, remove and drain. Coat the leeks in the dressing then roll in the seeds until they are evenly coated.

Place the leeks on a baking tray and cook in the oven for about 10 to 15 minutes.

Hot Vegetable Stew

This is yet another recipe that can be altered according to taste and what vegetables are available. If you are not a fan of hot food you can always eat it cold the next morning, or just omit the spices.

Serves 4

Ingredients

2 tbs of oil
1 onion, peeled and chopped
2 cloves of garlic, peeled and finely chopped
1 pepper, deseeded and sliced
2 courgettes sliced
1 leek, sliced
1 tin of chopped tomatoes
3 potatoes, peeled and diced
1 small can of sweetcorn
4 oz (100g) of cooked green lentils
1 green chilli pepper, chopped
Dash of tabasco sauce
1 pint (600ml) vegetable stock
2 tsp of mixed herbs
Salt
Pepper

Heat the oil in a large casserole dish, then fry the onions and garlic adding the chilli and tabasco, for 3 to 4 minutes. Then add the courgettes, leeks and peppers and gently fry for a further 10 minutes. Then add the stock and the remaining ingredients. Bring to the boil then simmer for 30 minutes.

Aubergine Bake

Serves 4

Ingredients

2 tbs of oil
1 large aubergine, thinly sliced
2 onions, peeled and chopped
2 cloves of garlic, chopped
5 oz (125g) pot of natural yoghurt
1 tin of chopped tomatoes
1 tbs of tomato purée
1 tsp of dried oregano
3 oz (75g) of grated cheddar cheese
1 oz (25g) of white breadcrumbs
Salt
Pepper

Heat the oil in a frying pan and add the aubergine slices. It is best to cook it in stages because only the bottom of the pan needs to be covered at any one time. Fry the aubergine until it has softened and slightly browned, then place on kitchen paper to absorb the oil. After cooking all the aubergine, remove it and fry the onion and garlic for 5 minutes.

The next stage is to add the tomato, tomato purée, oregano and seasoning. Bring to the boil, then simmer for 10 minutes before stirring in the yoghurt.

Using a greased ovenproof dish, arrange the aubergine then the tomato sauce in alternate layers. Continue this until the top layer is of aubergine. Cover the top with breadcrumbs and cheese.

Bake at Gas Mark 4 (350 °F, 180 °C), for around 30 minutes. Serve with rice or potatoes.

Other vegetables can be added, such as peppers or courgettes.

Stuffed Peppers

Serves 4

Ingredients
2 tbs of olive oil
4 peppers
1 onion, peeled and chopped
1 clove of garlic, peeled and finely chopped
1 tin of chopped tomatoes
2 tsp of tomato purée
4 oz (100g) mushrooms
Glass of red wine
1 tbs of chopped parsley
1 tsp of chopped rosemary
Dash of lemon juice
2 tbs of breadcrumbs
Salt
Pepper

Cut the tops off the peppers and remove the seeds, then place in boiling water for 3 to 4 minutes. Remove and plunge in cold water.

Heat the oil in a large saucepan and gently fry the onion and garlic for a few minutes. Add the other ingredients, bring to the boil and then simmer for 10 minutes. Fill the peppers with the mixture, replace the lid of the pepper and bake in the oven for 35 minutes on Gas Mark 6 (425 °F, 220 °C).

Pasta

Many students exist on a diet that is about as inspiring as some of the lectures they have to attend. Pasta is a popular choice for students, though this is probably something to do with the fact that it is cheap and is difficult to burn (I didn't say it was impossible). *Alphabetti Spaghetti* is also of enormous educational benefit for students, the more literate of whom are often able to spell rude words on their plates, much to the amusement of their less talented chums.

Pasta comes in various guises, and it is usually unimportant which type is used if it is being served with a sauce. The Italians are very keen on vegetarian food so there are many wonderful recipes in which to indulge.

I will start with the most simple of all Italian recipes, which is also one of the most delicious.

Pasta with Garlic and Oil

This is often referred to as 'poor man's pasta' . . . maybe it should be renamed 'student's pasta'? Olive oil is a must: don't be tempted to use vegetable oil which will taste disgusting.

Serves 4

Ingredients

8 tbs of olive oil
14oz (400g) spagehtti
3 cloves of garlic, peeled and crushed
Salt
Pepper

Cook the spaghetti according to the instructions on the packet. Whilst the pasta is cooking crush the garlic and mix it togther with the oil in a small bowl.

When the pasta is cooked, drain thoroughly and mix in the oil and garlic. Season well and serve immediately. For those of you who really love garlic add as many cloves as you dare.

If you're after a little more power try adding half a small red chilli pepper or a dash of tabasco sauce.

Parsley and Pasta

After coming home from lectures (that's if you got out bed in the first place) and having watched the daily dose of inspiring chat shows , this is a dish that can be prepared quickly and cheaply.

Serves 2

Ingredients

6 oz (150g) of wholemeal pasta shells
1 blob of butter or margarine
1 or 2 oz (25 or 50g) of cheddar cheese, grated
Lots of fresh parsley, roughly chopped
Salt
Pepper

Boil the pasta until it goes soft, then drain. Add the butter and allow it to melt. Add the salt, pepper, cheese and parsley, and toss until evenly distributed, then serve immediately.

Spaghetti with Tomato and Basil

Although a bottle of ketchup can help to obliterate the taste of some concoctions your friends might offer you, it is not what I had in mind for this recipe.

Serves 2

Ingredients

2 tbs olive oil
8 oz (225g) spaghetti
1 small onion, peeled and chopped
2 cloves of garlic, peeled and chopped
1 14oz (400g) tin of chopped tomatoes
6 basil leaves
Pinch of sugar
Salt
Pepper

Heat the oil in a saucepan, then fry the onions and garlic for 5 minutes or until they have softened. Add the other ingredients and cook for 15 to 20 minutes. Whilst the sauce is cooking, prepare the spaghetti according to the instructions on the packet. When the sauce is cooked pour into a blender and give it a whizz.

Drain the pasta and mix thoroughly with the sauce. Grated parmesan can be sprinkled on top if required.

Tagliatelli with Spinach and Walnuts

Serves 4

Ingredients

14 oz (400g) tagliatelli
1 lb (500g) fresh spinach
2 oz (50g) chopped walnuts
4 tbs of grated parmesan
2 tbs of fromage frais
Salt
Pepper

Whilst the pasta is cooking prepare the spinach. It is preferable to use young spinach leaves as the stalks are nice and soft. Wash the spinach and drain. Place in a deep pan and cook gently for a minute or two, stirring a couple of times. Remove the spinach from the pan, drain and then chop roughly.

Drain the pasta when it is cooked. Stir in the spinach, walnuts, parmesan, and fromage frais, then season. Heat through for a minute, then serve immediately.

Spaghetti with Gorgonzola

Serves 4

Ingredients

1 lb (500g) spaghetti
1 tbs walnuts, roughly chopped
2 oz (50g) butter
4 oz (100g) gorgonzola cheese
5 fl oz (150ml) single cream
Salt
Pepper

In a heavy saucepan melt the butter and then add the gorgonzola. Cook gently, stirring until the cheese has melted. It is essential that you do not have the heat too high. When the cheese has melted add the cream and cook gently for 5 minutes.

Remove from the heat and add the walnuts, then season.

Cook the pasta according to the instructions on the packet. Drain the pasta when cooked. Briefly reheat the sauce and mix in with the pasta, then eat with gusto.

Penne with Mushroom Sauce

Serves 4

Ingredients

1 tbs olive oil
14 oz (400g) penne
8 oz (100g) mushrooms
2 cloves of garlic, peeled and chopped
2 tbs fresh parsley

Clean the mushrooms, removing the stalks, then finely chop. Cook the pasta according to the instructions on the packet. Whilst the pasta is cooking, heat the oil in a large saucepan. Add the mushrooms and garlic and fry gently for five minutes.

When the pasta is cooked, drain and stir in the mushrooms and parsley. If it is a little dry, add a bit of butter or a little olive oil.

Rigatoni with Fresh Herbs

Serves 4

Ingredients

1 lb (500g) rigatoni
6 tbs of olive oil
1 clove of garlic, peeled and finely chopped
1 oz (25g) chopped fresh parsley
1 oz (25g) chopped fresh chives
1 oz (25g) chopped fresh basil
1 tbs rosemary leaves, finely chopped
Salt
Pepper

Cook the pasta according to the instructions on the packet. When cooked drain and then return to the pan with the herbs, oil, garlic and seasoning. Cook gently for a couple of minutes then serve immediately.

Fruit and Nut Pasta

The pine nuts and the sultanas are an unusual combination but you will find it delicious.

Serves 4

Ingredients

8 tbs of olive oil
14 oz (400g) of pasta
2 cloves of garlic, peeled and finely chopped
2 oz (50g) of sultanas
2 oz (50g) of pine kernels
Pepper

Cook the pasta of your choice according to the instructions on the packet. Drain the pasta and place in a serving bowl. Pour the oil over the pasta then stir in the garlic, pine kernels and sultanas. Season using lots of fresh ground pepper then serve immediately. Parmesan can be added on top if required.

Lasagne

As classicly Italian as Lambrettas, sunglasses, and the Mafia, this dish should make you feel as if you are sitting in a street café in Rome, surrounded by fine Roman architecture, sipping Chianti and flicking away the persistent flies.

Serves 4

Ingredients

2 tbs of oil
1 large onion, peeled and chopped
1 red pepper, deseeded and chopped
1 green pepper, deseeded and chopped
1 clove of garlic, peeled and finely chopped
1 leek finely chopped
2 courgettes finely sliced
1 tin of chopped tomatoes
2 tbs of tomato purée
2 tsp of oregano
1 packet of lasagne pasta (no pre-cooking required type)
Salt
Pepper

For the cheese sauce:

1 oz (25g) of butter
2 oz (50g) of flour
1 pint (600ml) of milk
6 oz (150g) of cheese, grated

Heat the oil in a large saucepan and add the onion and garlic. Cook for 5 minutes, then stir in the leek, peppers and courgette, fry gently for another 3 minutes or so. Add the tomatoes, purée, oregano and seasoning. Bring to the boil then simmer for a further 20 minutes. While the vegetable sauce is simmering prepare the cheese sauce.

Melt the butter in a saucepan and add the flour, stirring constantly. Remove from the heat and add the milk in stages. Then bring to the boil and add the cheese, saving a bit for the top. Simmer for 3 or 4 minutes. Add more flour if the sauce refuses to thicken, and shout at it if necessary.

Grease a shallow baking dish, then add a layer of tomato sauce, a layer of lasagne, a layer of cheese sauce, a layer of lasagne, and so on, making sure to end up with cheese sauce, sprinkle the loose cheese on top.

Bake in a preheated oven for around 25 minutes at Gas Mark 6 (425 °F, 220 °C).

Suppers and Snacks

Egg Hubble-bubble

Serves 1 to 2

Ingredients

4 potatoes, boiled
Any other vegetables
Butter or margarine
Cheese
4 eggs, lightly beaten and seasoned

Dice the potato, then fry it with any other vegetables you may have (eg. mushrooms, tomato, peas) in butter or margarine. When cooked, pour in the eggs and sprinkle with grated cheese. Cook very slowly with a plate or lid over the top, until the eggs are set.

Nachos

This is a quick and easy recipe that is perfect for any occasion.

Serves 4

Ingredients

2 tbs of oil
2 cloves of garlic, peeled and finely chopped
2 tsp of chilli powder
1 large onion, peeled and chopped
1 tin of chopped tomatoes
1 large bag of tortilla chips
4 oz (100g) grated cheese
1 tbs of tomato purée
1 green pepper, deseeded and finely chopped
Salt
Pepper

Heat the oil in a large saucepan, then fry the onion and garlic for about 3 to 4 minutes. Add the chilli powder and the green pepper and cook for another couple of minutes. Then add the tomatoes, tomato purée and seasoning and cook for about 15 minutes. The sauce has to be well reduced otherwise it will make the chips soggy.

Whilst the sauce is cooking arrange the tortilla chips in a ceramic dish. When the sauce is ready, pour over the chips and finally cover with cheese. Then place under a hot grill until the cheese has melted – enjoy.

Spanish Omelette

As there are numerous variations on this meal, don't hold yourself back with what you add.

Serves 4

Ingredients

4 eggs
1 potato, cooked for 10 minutes and chopped
2 tomatoes, sliced
1 oz (25g) of peas
1 onion, peeled and chopped
Mixed herbs
Salt
Pepper

Beat the eggs, season, add the vegetables and pour into a flan dish. Bake at Gas Mark 6 (425 °F, 220 °C) for 15 to 20 minutes or until the mixture ceases to be runny. If you prefer the onions to be a little more cooked, fry them first for a few minutes.

Serve with a green salad.

Onion Omelette

Serves 1 to 2

Ingredients

1 oz (25g) of butter
2 or 3 eggs
1 medium-sized onion, peeled and chopped.
Salt
Pepper

Melt the butter in a pan and fry the onions for a couple of minutes. Beat the eggs then add to the pan and cook as above.

Eggs

When choosing eggs there are a number of options. Battery-farmed eggs account for the majority of egg production but if possible, it is preferable to buy free-range eggs or barn eggs. Unfortunately, free range eggs are still a bit more expensive than battery-farmed, but it is worth paying the extra as they come from happy chickens and have lovely deep coloured yolks and definitely have more flavour due to the chicken's diet.

Many egg producers are now stamping (gently) a date on the egg.

If you have an egg that is not stamped and you think it may be stale then a qiuck test to try is to break the egg onto a small plate. If the egg is stale the yolk will be flat and the two layers of egg white will have merged. If in doubt it is best to throw it away. This is a rule that should be adhered to with any food.

Eggy Bread

Serves 2

Ingredients
3 eggs
4 tbs of milk
Slices of bread without the crusts
2 tbs of oil
Pepper

Beat the eggs and the milk together and season. Heat the oil in a frying pan. Dip a slice of bread in the egg mixture and then fry for a couple of minutes on each side.

Egg and Cheese Ramekins

Serves 1

Ingredients

2 oz (50g) of grated cheese
1 egg
1 tomato
Salt
Pepper

Grease a small ovenproof dish, preferably a ramekin dish or one that is about 3 inches (7.5cm) in diameter. Put grated cheese in the bottom of the dish and up the sides. Place in a slice of tomato and then the egg, trying not to break the yolk. Add the seasoning and cover with another slice of tomato and more grated cheese.

Bake in the oven for about 15 minutes at Gas Mark 4 (350 °F, 180 °C) or until the eggs are set.

Scrambled Egg

Serves 2

Ingredients

3 eggs
I oz (25g) of butter
4 tbs of milk
Pepper

Beat the eggs in a bowl and add the milk and pepper. Melt the butter in a saucepan and add the egg mixture. Stir the mixture as it thickens. Don't have the heat up too high, or else the egg will burn and stick to the pan.

Serve on top of hot buttered toast.

Poached Egg

Ingredients

I egg per person
Butter or margarine

If you happen to have a 'poaching ring' then put a nob of butter in and add the egg. Cook for about 4 minutes, according to taste.

There is a more traditional way of poaching eggs: boil some water in a saucepan, then having broken an egg into a cup or mug, slide it into the water. Only put one egg in at a time!

Fried Egg

Ingredients

1 egg
2 tbs of oil

Pour some oil in a frying pan, preferably non-stick. Don't let the fat get too hot, otherwise the egg will stick to the pan and bubble. Crack the egg on the side of the pan and plop the insides into the oil. Fry gently for about 3 minutes, basting occasionally. If you like your eggs American style (sunny side down), fry both sides of the egg.

Desserts

As a child it was the desserts that proved to be my weakness: anything with obscene amounts of chocolate and cream was shovelled down in amazing quantities. Those days of care-free eating are now over, replaced by that unfortunate phenomenon whereby you stop growing taller and start growing outwards instead.

Gooseberry Fool

Sometimes the gooseberries bought from supermarkets are quite sensible, but they can be made to look foolish by sticking small paper hats on them.

Serves 4

Ingredients

1 lb (500g) fresh gooseberries
10fl oz (300ml) double cream
6 oz (150g) castor sugar

Prepare the gooseberries by washing and removing any stalks and hats. Place in a saucepan without any water and simmer until they are tender. This should take about 15 minutes. When cooked, remove from the heat and leave for about five minutes to cool.

When the gooseberries have cooled place in a liquidizer with the sugar and blend. Beat the cream in a large bowl until it is nice and thick, then stir in the gooseberries. This can either be served in individual bowls or kept in the large bowl. Before serving, refrigerate, for at least an hour.

Fruit Salad

Not even a hint of chocolate.

Serves 4

Ingredients

1 banana
2 oranges
1 apple
2 oz (50g) grapes
4 oz (100g) of strawberries
Juice of 1 lemon
2 tbs of sugar
½ pint (150ml) of water

The above ingredients are just a guideline. You can use any fruit that is available or affordable. The given quantities will serve about 4 small bowls.

Wash all fruit before starting. Put the lemon juice and sugar in a mixing bowl and mix together. Cut the apple into quarters, remove the core and chop into small pieces.

Peel the oranges using a sharp knife, making sure all the pips are removed. Cut into segments, cutting between the membranes.

Cut the grapes in half and remove the pips. Peel the banana and cut into slices.

Skin and quarter the pear, then core it and chop into small pieces. The strawberries should be hulled (that means remove the green bit at the top), and cut in half.

Put all the fruit in the bowl with the lemon juice, sugar, and water, and mix thoroughly.

Serve either on its own or with cream.

Pears in Red Wine

Serves 4

Ingredients

4 pears
4 oz (100g) sugar
¼ pint (150ml) red wine
¼ pint (150ml) water
Pinch of cinnamon
1 oz (25g) browned almond flakes

Put the wine, water, sugar and cinnamon in a large saucepan and heat gently until the sugar has dissolved.

Peel the pears, trying not to damage the fruit, and leave the stalks on. Place the pears in the wine and simmer for about 20 minutes or until they are soft. When the pears are cooked remove from the pan and place in a serving dish. Reduce the wine sauce by boiling rapidly. It should develop a syrupy consistency. Pour the wine over the pears and when cool, chill in the fridge. Before serving sprinkle with almonds and serve with cream.

Ricotta and Raspberry Crunch

A delicious summer pudding that does not have to be made with raspberries, you could use strawberries, bananas or grapes. Another alternative is to use toasted pine nuts instead of the almonds.

Serves 4

Ingredients

12 oz (300g) ricotta cheese
8 oz (225g) fresh raspberries
Toasted almonds
Runny honey

Divide the ricotta into 4 bowls and arrange the raspberries around the edge of the cheese. Put about a tablespoon of honey on top of the cheese and then sprinkle with the toasted almonds. If you find that is a little bitter, either add more honey or dust with castor sugar.

Baked Apples

Serves 1

Ingredients

1 large cooking apple per person
Mincemeat
Brown sugar
Butter

Remove the cores from the apples and stand them in an ovenproof dish. Fill the hole in the apple with mincemeat and a teaspoon of brown sugar. Add a nob of butter on top. Put enough water in the dish to cover the bottom of the apples. Bake at Gas Mark 4 (350 °F, 180 °C) for about an hour.

After an hour test the apple with a skewer. It should be soft, but not too much. Serve with cream or ice cream.

Raspberry Brûlé

Serves 4

Ingredients

8 oz (225g) of fresh raspberries
½ pint (300ml) of double cream
6 oz (150g) of demerara sugar or golden granulated

Place the raspberries in a shallow heatproof dish. Whip the cream until thick, (but not too stiff) and spread over the raspberries.

Sprinkle sugar over the cream, covering it completely.

Preheat the grill and then place the brûlé under the grill, until it is dark and bubbling.

Remove from the grill and cool. Chill in the fridge for a couple of hours.

A cheaper version could be made using sliced banana.

Croissant Pudding

Serves 4

Ingredients

5 croissants
½ pint (300ml) of milk
2 oz (50g) of castor sugar
2 egg yolks
2 oz (50g) of raisins
Vanilla essence
Ground cinnamon
Brown sugar
Butter

Cut the croissants in half lengthways. Butter one side and put to the side. Beat the egg yolks, castor sugar and milk, add two drops of vanilla essence, then put aside. Grease an ovenproof dish and place a layer of croissants on the bottom, then sprinkle with raisins. Continue this until all the croissants are used up. Don't put too many raisins on the final layer as they are liable to burn.

Briefly beat the milk mixture, then pour over the croissants. Sprinkle with cinnamon. Leave to soak for at least 30 minutes.

Whilst the croissants are soaking preheat the oven to Gas Mark 4 (180 °C, 350 °F).

Sprinkle a thin layer of brown sugar over the top of the dish then place in the middle of the oven for 20 minutes. Remove from the oven, add some more sugar and return to the oven for a further 20 minutes.

Poached Peaches

Serves 4

Ingredients

Tin of peach halves
½ oz (15g) of butter or margarine
2 tbs of brown or golden granulated sugar
1 tbs of brandy or whisky, optional

Drain the syrup from the peaches, reserving a small amount. Melt the butter in a saucepan. Add the peaches with the syrup and sugar.

Heat gently for about 5 minutes then stir in the booze, if desired.

If you have any flaked almonds or nuts, a few of these toasted and sprinkled on top taste good.

Baked Bananas

I have no doubt that if you not tried this recipe, after tasting it you will be smitten. Make sure that you use dark chocolate as milk chocolate is just not the same.

Serves 4

Ingredients

4 large bananas
4 oz (100g) dark chocolate

Take a sharp knife and make a sharp incision through the skin of the banana from end to end. Gently peel the skin apart and make another incision the length of the banana. Be careful not to pierce the other side of the skin.

Break the chocolate into small pieces and then insert the chocolate in the cavity. Close the edges of the banana skin together then wrap in a foil parcel.

Place the bananas in the oven on its highest setting and cook until they have softened through to the centre and the chocolate has melted. Serve with thick double cream.

Baked Bananas II

Serves 1

Ingredients

1 banana
Brown or golden granulated sugar
Lemon juice

Peel the banana and place it on a piece of foil, shiny side uppermost. Squeeze the lemon juice over the banana, sprinkle with brown sugar, and loosely wrap up.

Place the bananas in the oven on its highest setting and cook until they have softened through to the centre.

Treacle Tart

This can be served hot or cold, with cream or ice cream or on its own.

Serves 4

Ingredients

4 oz (100g) plain flour
2 oz (50g) fresh white breadcrumbs
3 tbs water
2 oz (50g) butter
12 tbs golden syrup
2 tsp grated lemon rind
Salt

Add a pinch of salt to the flour and sieve. Cut the fat into small pieces and rub them into the flour until the mixture resembles fine breadcrumbs. Add a tablespoon of water at a time until a firm dough is produced. Cover a clean surface or pastry board with a sprinkling of flour. Roll out the pastry so that there is enough to cover the bottom and the sides of a 8-inch (20cm) flan dish. Mix the syrup, breadcrumbs and lemon juice together then spoon into the flan case.

Bake for about 25 minutes at Gas Mark 6 (425 °F, 220 °C), until golden.

Biscuits and Cakes

The emphasis of this book is on preparing main meals rather than cakes and biscuits, as cooking main meals will be of more use. However, teatime comes about every afternoon, usually at about teatime, so an introduction to basic cake-making is included. There is nothing fancy or difficult — I will leave that to others. Cakes are like students — they can often fail to rise for no apparent reason, but you can't go too far wrong with a good old Victoria sponge.

Victoria Sponge

The Victoria sponge is easy to make and if eaten whilst still warm it is hard to beat. As an alternative add cream between the layers.

Ingredients

4 oz (100g) of self-raising flour
4 oz (100g) of margarine
4 oz (100g) of castor sugar
2 eggs, beaten
Jam

(Two 7-inch sandwich tins are needed)

Mix together the sugar and margarine until they are smooth in texture. Gradually add the eggs to the mixture, then fold in the flour. Divide the mixture between the two baking tins (these need to be greased first, which means wiping the inside with a piece of greaseproof paper covered with margarine). Make sure that the tops of the cakes are level, then bake in the oven for 20 minutes or so at Gas Mark 5 (400 °F, 200 °C).

The way to see if a cake is cooked is to stick a skewer or a knitting needle (if you happen to have one handy) in the centre of the sponge. If bits of the mixture are stuck to it when it is drawn out, it needs to be cooked a little longer. If the skewer comes out clean, the cake is ready.

Now turn the cakes out of the tins onto a wire rack (look in the grill pan for one). Once cooled, spread a layer of jam over one half, sandwich the other one on top, and sprinkle with castor sugar.

Carob Cake

Ingredients

4 oz (100g) wholemeal self-raising flour
4 oz (100g) margarine
4 oz (100g) sugar
2 eggs
2 oz (50g) carob powder
2 tsp mixed spice

Preheat the oven to Gas Mark 4 (180 °C, 350 °F)

Beat the margarine and sugar together until smooth: it's worth softening the margarine before you do this. Mix in the eggs then add the flour, mixed spice and carob powder. Using a wooden spoon combine until all the ingredients are blended together.

Grease a shallow baking tin then spoon the mixture in evenly. Bake for 20-25 minutes. When cool cut into squares.

Chocolate Crunch

Ingredients

4 oz (100g) digestive biscuits, crushed
4 oz (100g) rich tea biscuits, crushed
4 oz (100g) butter
3 oz (75g) golden syrup
1 oz (25g) cocoa powder
6 oz (100g) plain chocolate
Icing sugar

Using a piece of greaseproof paper with a small amount of butter on wipe the inside of a shallow baking tin. Using a can of WD40 would be quicker but it probably wouldn't taste as good. Melt the butter in a saucepan then add the syrup and cocoa, mix together then add the crushed biscuits. Remove from the heat. Stir the mixture thoroughly so that the biscuit crumbs are evenly coated. Transfer the biscuit mixture into the tin and press down the mixture using a back of a spoon and leave to cool.

To melt the chocolate, place a Pyrex bowl on top of a pan of simmering water. Don't put too much water in the saucepan as there is a chance the water might boil over the edge. Place the chocolate in the bowl and let it melt. When the chocolate has completely melted, remove the bowl from the heat using a pair of oven gloves and pour the chocolate over the biscuit mixture. Spread the chocolate so there is an even coating. Allow to cool then cut into squares or slices. Dust with icing sugar. If the weather is warm they can be kept in the fridge to stop them from melting.

N.B. To crush the biscuits, put them in a clean bag, tie the ends and bash with a rolling pin.

Rock Buns

There are several alternatives to this recipe: jazz buns, classical buns, and the ever popular easy listening buns.

Ingredients

8 oz (225g) of self-raising flour
4 oz (100g) of margarine
3 oz (75g) of currants or raisins
A pinch of nutmeg
3 oz (75g) of sugar
1 egg, beaten
2 tbs of milk
A pinch of salt

Mix the flour, nutmeg and salt together. Then rub the flour and margarine together until they look like breadcrumbs. The next stage is to add the currants, sugar, egg and milk. The mixture should be fairly firm.

Grease a baking tray with some margarine. Mould the mixture into small lumps and place on the baking tray.

Bake for 15 to 20 minutes, Gas Mark 6 (425 °F, 220 °C).

Chocolate Cake

Ingredients

6 oz (150g) of self-raising flour
6 oz (150g) of margarine
6 oz (150g) of castor sugar
3 eggs
1 ½ oz (40g) of cocoa
1 ½ tbs of water

(For the icing)

8 oz (225g) of icing sugar
4 oz (100g) of plain cooking chocolate
1 ½ oz (40g) of butter/margarine
2 tbs of warm water

Place the sugar and the margarine in a large mixing bowl and mix together, using either a wooden spoon or an electric mixer (which will save time). Add the eggs, one at a time.

In a separate bowl, mix the flour and the cocoa powder together, then add it to the creamed mixture. Continue mixing, adding water until a soft dropping consistency is achieved.

Divide the mixture equally between two 7-inch (17cm) sandwich tins. Bake in the oven at Gas Mark 5 (400 °F, 200 °C) for 25 to 30 minutes.

Test the cake with a skewer. If the mixture sticks to it, the cake needs a few more minutes in the oven.

When the cakes are ready, turn them out of their tins onto a wire rack (if available). Melt the chocolate by placing it in a basin and putting that over the top of a saucepan of boiling water. Be careful not to let the water boil over the top of the saucepan into the chocolate.

After the chocolate has melted, allow to cool. Cream together the butter and half the icing sugar, then add half the melted chocolate. Mix, and spread over one side of the cake, then 'sandwich' the two together.

The rest of the chocolate is used to make the icing on the top. Add the water and sugar to the chocolate, and spoon onto the top of the cake. Spread the icing around using a palette knife that has been dipped in hot water (this helps to spread the icing and stop it sticking to the knife).

Strawberry Buns

Ingredients

8 oz (225g) of self-raising flour
4 oz (100g) of castor sugar
3 oz (75g) of margarine
1 egg, beaten
1 tbs of milk
Strawberry jam
A pinch of salt

Rub the margarine and flour together using your fingertips, until the mixture resembles breadcrumbs. Add the sugar, salt, egg, and milk, and mix well. The mixture should be quite stiff.

Grease a baking tray, then shape the mixture into twelve balls and place on the tray. Make a little hole on the top of each and fill with a teaspoon of jam.

Bake in the oven on Gas Mark 7 (425 °F, 220 °C) for about 20 minutes.

Flapjacks

Ingredients

8 oz (225g) of porridge oats
4 oz (100g) of margarine
3 oz (75g) of sugar
4 tbs of golden syrup
A pinch of salt

Melt the margarine in a large saucepan, then add the syrup and leave over a low heat for a couple of minutes. Remove from the heat and add the sugar, salt and oats. Mix thoroughly using a wooden spoon, making sure all the oats are covered with syrup.

Grease a shallow baking tray and evenly spoon in the mixture. Cook for 20 to 30 minutes at Gas Mark 4 (350 °F, 180 °C). After cooking, cut the flapjacks into bars before they cool.

Scones

There's nothing more British than a traditional cream tea. Except perhaps rain. And driving on the left. Oh, and a system of government that gives some of its power to unelected, inbred aristocrats who have lost control of most of their senses. Anyway, cream teas, with thick scones oozing homemade jam and thick clotted cream, are equal to anything found in a French pâtisserie, and although they might not look as elegant they taste delicious.

Ingredients

8 oz (225g) of self-raising flour
2 oz (50g) of margarine
¼ pint (150ml) of milk
A pinch of salt

Mix the flour and salt together. The flour is supposed to be sieved, but it's a bit time-consuming and doesn't make much difference anyway. Cut the margarine into small cubes and add them to the flour. Rub the mixture using your fingers, continuing until the result looks like breadcrumbs.

Add the milk and stir in using the blade of a knife to form a soft dough. Roll out the mixture on a floured board until it is about ½ an inch (1.5cm) thick. Cut into rounds using a biscuit cutter or a glass.

Grease a baking tray and place some scones on it, leaving enough room for them to rise. Brush some milk over the top of the scones for that smooth and shiny finish.

Bake in the oven for 10 to 15 minutes at Gas Mark 7 (450 °F, 230 °C).

Cheese Scones

As for above, but stir in 4 oz (100g) of cheese before adding the milk.

Fruit Scones

As for plain scones, but stir in 1 oz (25g) of sugar and 2 oz (50g) of dried fruit (sultanas, currants etc.)

Batters

Yorkshire Pudding

Serves 4

Ingredients

4 oz (100g) of plain flour
1 egg, beaten
½ pint (300ml) of milk, or milk and water
Oil
A pinch of salt

Mix the salt and flour in a mixing bowl, then make a 'well' in the flour and add the egg. Mix together carefully, adding the milk little by little. Beat the mixture for a few minutes until it is smooth. Pour a teaspoon of oil into the individual patty tins, then add 2 tablespoons of the mixture into each. Bake for about 15 minutes or until they have risen and browned.

Pancakes

Serves 4

Ingredients

4 oz (100g) of plain flour
1 egg
½ pint (300ml) of milk
A pinch of salt
Butter
Sugar (or any other topping)

Put the flour and salt in a bowl and add the egg into the middle. Pour in about a third of the milk. Stir gently, adding a little more milk in the process. Beat the mixture thoroughly, then add the rest of the milk. Stir well, then pour into a jug.

Melt a small piece of butter in a frying pan, then add a couple of tablespoons of the batter. Tip the frying pan to spread the mixture evenly. Fry until the underside is brown, then toss the pancake.

Scrape the mess from the dropped pancake off the floor, then start again. This time, when the underside is brown, turn it over with a fish slice or a knife and cook the other side.

Tip the finished pancake onto a plate and cover with lemon juice and sugar.

Booze

This is one subject that most students seem to have a natural ability to understand, and a great deal of time is given by students to gaining the most from this area of knowledge. Some of the recipes in this book contain wine, but often it is optional (they just taste better if you can afford it).

Wine

The standard offering at a dinner party tends to be wine. Normally guests will bring a bottle of wine with them, but buy a few bottles in case they don't.

The availability and consumption of wine is probably the highest it has ever been, which goes some way to explaining why it is no longer regarded as a snobbish drink.

My knowledge of wine is purely based on experimentation, which is probably the most enjoyable way to gain familiarity. Those who are already connoisseurs will probably find this section irrelevant.

Apart from the obvious wine growing countries like France, Germany, Spain and Portugal there are several countries that have made huge investments in vineyards, and have since become serious contenders in the wine market. The heavy investment, especially in America, has made use of new technology that has left the methods used by the French and other European countries looking somewhat dated.

The Australians have also come up with some excellent wines recently, many of which are very reasonably priced. Don't be put off by names like 'Seaview', I know it sounds more like a seaside guesthouse, but the taste is the important thing.

Choose whatever wine you prefer. It doesn't really matter

whether you serve red wine with fish or white wine with red meat. Just avoid serving red wine with white wine. One colour at a time is adequate.

Sangria

This famous Spanish punch is a real knockout, and is customarily drunk during the summer. A variety of fruit can be added according to personal preference. If you drink it in the sun you should be ready to enter the bull ring after only your third glass.

Ingredients

2 bottles chilled red wine
4 tbs Cognac
1 tbs castor sugar
¾ pint (450ml) chilled soda water
Sliced peach
Sliced strawberries
Slices apple
12 ice cubes

Find a large jug or bowl and place the fruit in the bottom. Pour the wine, Cognac and sugar over the fruit and leave for an hour. Then pour in the soda and add the ice cubes.

Mulled Wine

Good after bonfire night or at Christmas.

Ingredients

1 bottle of red wine
4 to 6 tsp of sugar
The rind of 1 orange or lemon
2-inch stick of cinnamon
A blade of mace
2 cloves
Slices of orange/lemon for serving

Heat the wine and sugar, but do not allow to boil. Then add the orange and spices. Strain and serve.

Booze-ups

Few students need to learn anything more about this familiar subject. A booze-up may be pre-arranged, or may follow quite naturally from the dinner party. A common scenario is for the wine/lager to run out soon after the meal, resulting in a mad rush to get to the off-licence before it shuts. This can be avoided with a little forward planning. Pool the house money (or dip into the week's kitty) and buy cheap alcohol from a large supermarket. This should save a bit of money and panic in the long run.

Before a booze-up takes place it is important to remove all objects that might suffer its effects: neighbours, landlords, televisions, the entire house. In fact, it is far better to hold it in someone else's house or on a beach etc. A surprising number of videos, CD players, and half-written essays suffer untimely demises in the hands of spilt beer at these events, so take care.

Punches

These things are produced in bulk, and are not intended for the lone drinker. The quantities involved are such that a plastic beer-brewing barrel is probably the best thing to mix it in. Or the bath. Coloured effects can be obtained by using orange juice or Ribena.

Punches are another way to save money at a booze-up. Strong drinks will go further when they are mixed with orange juice or lemonade or whatever. But some punches can be deadly, so check exactly what is going into the mixture, preferably sticking to a pre-agreed plan or recipe. The completed punch can then be poured back into its component bottles, so that everyone should have a litre or so to themselves.

Here's a couple of easy punches to get things swinging . . .

Rum Punch

Ingredients

1 pint (0.5 litre) of white rum
5 pints (2.5 litres) of orange juice
1 pint (0.5 litre) of grapefruit juice
Dash of grenadine
1 orange, sliced

Mix the above ingredients together and serve with paper umbrellas if required!

Put the gin, sugar and lemon juice in a shaker with the ice and give it a shake.

Strain into a tall glass and top up the glass with soda then add the slice of lemon.

Margarita

Most people have their own tequila story or nightmare – even a sniff of tequila can make me feel green.

Ingredients

1 measure tequila
½ measure triple sec
2 tbs lemon juice
Lemon rind
Salt
Ice

A short glass is preferable. Rub the rim of the glass with the lemon rind then dip in the salt. The idea is to a have light dusting of salt rather than a thick crust.

Put the tequila, triple sec, lemon juice and cracked ice into a shaker and give it your best Tom Cruise impression. Strain into a glass and enjoy.

Conclusion

I hope that you've managed to sustain yourself to reach the end of this book, and that it's given you an interest in cooking.

Good luck with all that studying and just remember you are unlikely ever to get the chance to lounge around most of the day watching 6 different American chat-shows, wear clothes that make you look like a refugee and be terribly right-on, so make the most of it.

Index